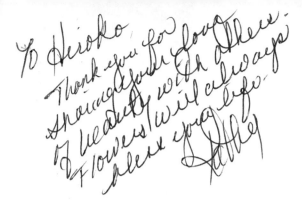

# Transformation Through Flowers
## *Spiritual and Physical Healing*

Kathleen Lemler, M.A.

**Expressions of Nature**
**Oxnard, California**

**Transformation Through Flowers Spiritual and Physical Healing**
by Kathleen Lemler

**Expressions of Nature**
1259 W. Gonzales Rd.
Oxnard, CA 93030

Copyright © 1993  Kathleen A. Lemler

Library of Congress Catalog Number:  93-070505

International Standard Book Number:  0-9635987-0-8

Flowers Arrangements by Kathleen Lemler
Illustrations of Flower Arrangements : Mary Ann Harris
Cover Design:  Mary Ann Harris
Cover Painting "Hibiscus" © Ken Goldman

Printed in the United States of America

*To my students
who grant me the privilege
of being their teacher*

# Table of Contents

# Preface

Arranging flowers in what has become known as the art form of Ikebana, began as a spiritual activity with a spiritual purpose. The transformative power of nature was recognized by the early Buddhist priests who created plant groupings for the temple altar as an offering to the Gods, and to ward off any evil spirits. It was a form of worship, and at the same time, a means of purifying the area by eliminating negative thoughts or forces in the vicinity.

Since early times, there has been a conscious recognition by many individuals of the flowers' ability to heal and transform. One such individual, Mokichi Okada, wrote an article in 1949 titled, "The Role of Flowers in Establishing Paradise on Earth." In it he speaks of the world's negativity being alleviated by the presence of flowers wherever there are people. It was his experience that flowers could impact people and environments, and would help to create an ideal world of truth, virtue, and beauty.

That flowers make a difference in people's lives has led to the increasing popularity of flower arranging, and to the practice of growing and arranging flowers in prisons and in various rehabilitation settings. After experiencing a transformation in myself through participation in Sangetsu flower arranging, and observing a similar phenomenon in others, I began to ask the questions, "How do flowers heal and transform?" and "What is it that is being healed that results in a change of attitude, character, and health?" I wanted to know how flowers are able to influence human life, and specifically, how the Sangetsu style of Ikebana works with the forces that effect a transformation.

My quest for understanding led me on a metaphysical search of philosophies from both the East and the West. The spiritual sciences of Mokichi Okada and Rudolf Steiner, along with the investigative experiences of Johann Wolfgang von Goethe, provided the greatest insight into how flowers heal. Others, including Dora van Gelder Kunz, Dorothy Maclean, Corrine Heline, and Gregory Conway, provided further understanding and inspiration.

This book is about healing and transformation through flowers in the way of Sangetsu. The information presented here can benefit all those interested in arranging flowers; in healing; in working in rehabilitation programs; or those who wish only to renew their relationship to nature and to self.

*This great nature is God's work of art. In every branch and flower God's skillful plan flows. We need only go out and choose what we like from His bounty. It is not necessary for us to "rearrange" nature; we just need to add a few touches. It is beautiful as it is, as it manifests life. The important thing to remember is not to destroy these life-filled flowers and branches, for through them we taste the joys of nature's offering.*

*Mokichi Okada*

*Chapter One*

## Sangetsu Philosophy and Guidelines

The Sangetsu School of Flower Arranging acknowledges the power of nature and its role in healing as presented by Mokichi Okada (1882-1955). Okada's philosophy, along with his desire to see each person become truly healthy and happy, provided the inspiration for the founding of the school on June 15, 1972 in Atami, Japan.

Mokichi Okada was a businessman, humanitarian, art collector, and artist who later became a spiritual leader. He was born into circumstances of poverty in the eastern part of Japan on December 23, 1882—the day following the winter solstice when daylight begins to gain over the darkness on the earth. Okada received a revelation in 1926 which included the cause and ways to overcome humankind's three scourges—disease, poverty, and conflict. He believed that art and beauty would play a significant role in transforming humanity and bringing about world peace. To this end, he established bringing about world peace. To this end, he established an art museum and created beautiful gardens that would serve as prototypes for future expansion of the arts, that all people might be inspired.

Okada's love for nature and beauty surfaced as a young child, planting small flower gardens and trees wherever his family moved in spite of their poverty. The family circumstances gradually improved, paving the way for Okada to develop a successful business designing and selling women's accessories. As a prosperous businessman, he could afford to have a master flower arranger come to his home. Okada stood behind and watched as the flowers were arranged. In this way he gleaned basic techniques in the art of Ikebana.

Okada was concerned that quite unusual arrangements devoid of life were becoming increasingly popular in Japan. His observation led him to state, "In this world today, things are becoming more and more unnatural, in contradiction to nature, such as artificially painted flowers. What I am going to do is stress the importance of preserving natural beauty."[1] As a spiritual leader, he began to make arrangements of his own expressing the inherent beauty of the flowers. It was his intention to write a book on flower arranging to awaken people to the laws of nature and their application in Ikebana. Unfortunately, Okada died before he accomplished this goal, but left guidelines by which to arrange flowers naturally. These guidelines have provided the foundation for the Sangetsu style of arranging.

Okada experienced the consciousness of nature as he observed and worked with plant materials (trees and flowers). He said, "If you believe that everything in nature has consciousness and treat it accordingly, you will not make any mistakes."[2] Okada was not implying that plants have the same consciousness as human beings, but that there is a life force that is responsive to circumstances and to human emotions and vibrations. A nursery foreman once told Okada that whenever he found a blossoming tree that did not bloom he would say, "If you do not produce blossoms this year, I am going to cut you down."[3] The tree, he related, would then invariably bloom. He gave another example of a tree that was given such love and attention by its caretaker that it grew to maturity about seven years sooner than expected.[4]

The love and reverence expressed toward plants, and the way in which they are handled is of utmost importance in flower arranging. There is a reciprocal energy that flows between the flowers and the individual, and out into the environment when an attitude of reverence is present. This energy, which facilitates healing and transformation, is enhanced when flowers are arranged with joy.

Okada experienced the joy of nature, and arranged flowers for his home and guests in that spirit. His arrangements were always an expression of his love for nature, and his desire to express its truth and beauty.

The Sangetsu motto of Jitsu, Jitsu, Kyo, or "two parts nature to one part technique," is based upon this attitude toward nature. The love and appreciation we feel for our materials is more important than the technique we use to arrange them. All art forms require technique and a step-by-step process in order to develop skills. According to the headmistress of the Sangetsu School, Itsuki Okada, "To give true life to flowers, to produce a beautiful flower arrangement, we must have knowledge, technique and practice."[5] Technique is necessary to understand the mechanics of flower placement, but the flowers themselves teach us how they wish to be arranged.

We can observe the growing patterns in nature, and place materials in an arrangement that reflects their natural beauty. "I never force any of the growths into particular shapes," said Okada, "but simply arrange them in their own natural forms as much as possible so they are and continue to look fresh and full of life."[6] Plant materials grow upright, at a slant, or horizontally to the right or left. Others have an appearance of lively motion or parallel lines. Plant materials also have a positive and negative aspect, the positive being the side which is most pleasing to the eye and expresses the material's greater beauty.

Flowers speak to us in many ways but initially they do this through their visible growth pattern. For example, flowers grow toward the sun, not looking down at the earth. Each has a unique beauty and line, and because plants have consciousness and vitality, they desire to be arranged to their best advantage. These natural lines and rhythms characteristic of the materials are expressed in Sangetsu arrangements.

Okada explained that flowers that have been handled only briefly will retain their natural vitality and will be able to adjust themselves in an arrangement if they have not been placed quite to their liking. I experienced this phenomenon once after completing a nageire arrangement (style using an upright container), and indeed, the flowers did move to display greater beauty than when I had arranged them.

Okada made flower arrangements in less than

five minutes. He attributed the freshness, longevity, and natural appearance of the flowers he arranged to the speed with which they were arranged. He taught that handling flowers too much or playing with them weakens their vitality.

In order to arrange flowers quickly and without unnecessary handling, it is important first to visualize the design to be made and to select a vase. The materials must then be cut and arranged with swift determination. The flowers will remain full of life and energy when cared for in this way.

Okada's arrangements were unusual in that he demonstrated the use of fewer flowers and varieties of flowers to be placed in one arrangement. He believed his style to be more effective, more artistic. "Arranging flowers is like painting a picture or making brush strokes with them. People give me compliments about my arrangements because I think I am drawing or painting pictures with my flowers."[7] He further stated, "You cannot make a good flower arrangement without the ability to appreciate pictures. To develop this artistic sense, you must constantly look at and study beautiful works of art."[8]

Observation of nature teaches us that flowers and other plant materials grow at a predetermined time of year and have a cycle of life that is peculiar to each. Okada said, "As a basic rule, it is most effective to use flowers that are at their best at the time. This is in accordance with the laws of nature."[9] It is in harmony with nature to use flowers in the season of their growth. It is at that time that they are the strongest and most beautiful, and the least expensive if you must buy them. However, due to the vacillating weather conditions (the extremes of which Okada attributes to the imbalance of human emotion) and green house technology, many varieties of plants now are grown out of their natural season and even year round.

The foliage during the seasons illustrates to us the breathing of the earth. According to Okada the earth breathes once a year.[10] The exhalation phase begins and is most intense in the spring during which time there is an abundance of plant growth. The exhaling of the earth continues through summer to its peak, and then it begins to inhale. At this time, in the early fall, the plants wither and the trees lose their leaves, leaving Mother Earth with a different array of vegetation for this season. By using materials appropriate to the seasons we are in harmony with the earth and all of nature. We can display its beauty in the full glory of its color in a work of art that is pleasing to both nature and humankind.

Creating a masterpiece with flowers is the intent of Sangetsu. To accomplish this the arrangement must embody balance and harmony. Balance is achieved in the flowers by utilizing both buds about to open and those closer to their bloom, and selecting branches that are in harmony in color and texture. All plant materials have a certain delicacy or strength, shape, and color which lends them to be arranged in a particular style and color of vase. The arrangement's placement in a room must also be considered as to space and color of surroundings and other art works present. A masterpiece of art is achieved through the overall harmony of flowers, vase, and space. Okada stated, "If everything is harmonious, the viewer feels a wonderfully pleasant vibration and his appreciation of beauty and harmonious balance is enhanced or awakened."[11]

14

Okada taught that nature is truth; it is God's great art. In creating a floral masterpiece nature's truth and beauty are expressed and combined with human skill and artistic ability, balancing the spiritual and the physical. It is a goal of Sangetsu to balance these two principles through flower arrangement, and by doing so, provide a healing impulse that can change the world.

*Those who deeply love*
*And appreciate flowers,*
*Their grace, their beauty,*
*Must have hearts which truly must be*
*Equally as beautiful.[12]*

*Little flower--but if I could understand*
*What you are root and all, and all in all,*
*I should know what God and man is.*
*Tennyson*

*Chapter Two*

# Spiritual Energies and Form

The basic styles in Sangetsu Ikebana are expressed in the form of a scalene or asymmetrical triangle. The asymmetry creates depth and balance in the arrangement and allows all materials to be appreciated individually as well as collectively. The scalene triangle is made up of three main lines of varying heights placed at angles according to their natural line and rhythm (figure 1). Historically, these three lines have been called heaven, man, and earth, and symbolize man as standing between heaven and earth in the universal order. The philosophy of heaven, man, and earth was based on Confucian doctrine and took form in the following symbology: "Heaven, the tallest and principal line symbolizes 'the soul of all elements of life'; Man, secondary or intermediary line, 'the fundamental way by which all things become active'; and Earth, the shortest and tertiary line, 'the way in which all things take form.'"[1]

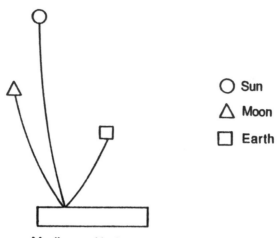

○ Sun
△ Moon
□ Earth

**Moribana Upright/Right Floral Figure**

**Moribana Horizontal/Left Floral Figure**

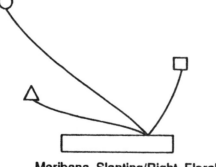

**Moribana Slanting/Right Floral Figure**

Figure 1

In the Sangetsu school these three lines are referred to as the sun, the moon, and the earth. They receive their names from the planetary sun, moon, and earth, but represent invisible spiritual energies emitted by these physical bodies. Okada Identified the spirit of fire, the spirit of water, and the spirit of soil as the energies which come from the sun, moon, and earth respectively.[2]

An explanation of the science of energies and its relationship to healing is offered through a diagrammatical placement of the sun, moon, and earth in a vertical line.[3] (figure 2). Okada describes these three levels in the following way:

> The spiritual plane is the plane of fire, with the sun at its center. The atmospheric plane is the plane of water, with the moon as its center. The physical plane is the plane of soil, with the earth as its center.[4]

The earth plane on which we live consists of both spirit and matter. Matter is solid and is easily seen on the physical plane. Atmosphere is filled with the element of water and is half-matter; the spirit of fire emitted from the sun is of a higher vibration and is considered non-matter according to Okada.[5]

These energies are more commonly known on the physical plane as the elements of oxygen (fire), hydrogen (water), and nitrogen (soil).[6] The invisible essence behind each element is not widely acknowledged, particularly the spirit of fire. We feel heat which is the result of the spirit of fire. Light is produced, says Okada, when the energies of fire and water unite.[7] We view physical light but spiritual light is invisible to most as it is a purer vibration. Okada states that by adding the energy of soil

19

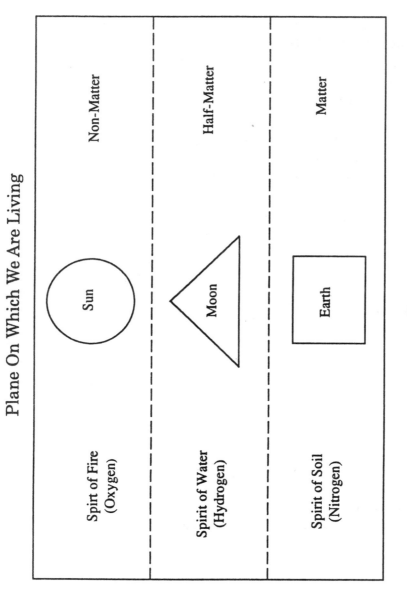

Plane On Which We Are Living

Figure 2

to the energies of fire and water, a light with wonderful healing powers is emitted.[8]

Being inseparably combined, the energies of fire, water and soil create currents that flow vertically, horizontally, and in all other directions. Through the combined energy emanating from these, everything comes into existence and realizes its growth.[9]

Okada referred to this phenomenon as the three-in-one-concept of the universe. These separate yet combined energies are paramount to sustaining life on the planet earth. Without fire everything on the planet would freeze; without water, it would explode; and without soil everything would crumble.[10]

A balance is created in the atmosphere due to the combination of the fire element flowing vertically and the water element flowing horizontally. This balance, however, can be upset by the negative thoughts and emotions that are sent forth by persons into the atmosphere, according to Okada. For example, the weather will become hotter if people lose their emotional equilibrium; colder if they lack love; or murky if they are complaining and resentful.[11]

Given the concept that everything comes into existence through the power of the three energies combined, it is reasonable to expect a visible correspondence in the human being. Okada views the human being as consisting of spirit, soul, and body. He describes the spirit or spiritual body as infinite and having eternal life, as opposed to the finite physical body which fulfills its purpose in one lifetime.[12] The soul is an intermediary principle between the spirit and body and, one in which, according to spiritual scientist, Dr. Rudolf Steiner

(1861-1925), the impulse for the activities of thinking, feeling, and willing arise.[13] The spirit, soul, and body embrace the elements of fire, water, and earth respectively.

The soul activities of thinking, feeling, and willing can also be seen to relate to fire, water, and earth. Our will is expressed in the form of activities and deeds that are carried out on the physical plane, which has to do with the spirit of soil. Emotions/feelings are similar to half-matter in that the inward activity of feeling is not necessarily known to anyone but the individual, but the expression of emotion can be observed, such as in crying, blushing, depression, etc. Thinking relates more to the spirit of fire or non-matter. A person's thoughts are more difficult to detect than feelings or will activities as they are invisible to most. It is through our thought processes, too, that we can raise ourself to higher realms of consciousness which have to do with the spirit.

The heart, lungs, and stomach are considered by Okada to be among the most important organs in the human body. The heart draws in the spirit of fire from the spiritual realm through pulsation, and thereby maintains the body's temperature; the lungs take in the spirit of water from the atmosphere through respiration, and assist in maintaining the body's moisture; the stomach absorbs the spirit of soil through the intake of food.[14]

Just how important these elements are to human life can be understood by viewing their withdrawal at death. As the spiritual body of the person separates from the physical body and returns to the spiritual realm, the heart stops pulsating and drawing in the spirit of fire, which causes the body temperature to drop and the body to become cold.[15] The spirit of water returns to the atmosphere when respiration ceases, causing the body's moisture to dry up.[16] As the stomach can no longer take in the spirit of soil through nutrients, the body becomes rigid.[17] At death, says Okada, "...fire returns to the spiritual plane, water returns to the atmospheric plane, and soil returns to the earth plane."[18]

While working as a nurse in hospitals, I witnessed the transition of several persons and can attest to the spiritual/physical phenomena as described by Okada. It was often apparent that a person was near death, not necessarily through his body which had been debilitated by illness, but through his eyes in which I could see a withdrawal of energy or life. Many nurses call this "the look of death." About the same time the extremities would become cold, generally starting at the feet and working up the body. This was a fairly accurate sign of impending death. Following the person's transition, the body would become stiff. At the time, I understood the process of death through these three visible signs: the energy withdrawal, the coldness and drying of body fluids, and later, rigidity. I had no knowledge of the spiritual forces behind this cycle of life. I now understand that there is a spiritual activity that precedes the physical phenomena.

These universal life energies find their pattern reflected on the earth and in the human being in various forms. A further microcosm can be seen in a Sangetsu flower arrangement. Utilizing the lines of the sun, moon, and earth, we create an arrangement demonstrating the three separate energies uniting into one from which a work of healing art will arise.

Okada said that a flower is already perfect in itself, and that it is a small prototype of the universe. I believe he was referring to the presence of all three spiritual energies in the flower. The spirit of fire is in the blossom, the spirit of water in the leaf, and the spirit of soil in the root. The flower, having the spirits of fire, water, and soil combined in its form, projects a wonderful healing light.

I believe this healing energy is demonstrated most strongly in Korinka, the advanced level in the Sangetsu school. Korinka's name states its purpose. It means "circles of light" and was chosen from one of Okada's calligraphies; Ko is light, Rin is circle.[19] Ka is the Japanese word for flower. The name was also inspired by a favorite artist of Okada's—Korin Ogata. The ideal is for Korinka arrangements to spread light and beauty in ever expanding circles, embracing peoples, cultures, and nations. An analogy given is the ripple effect of a pebble which has been thrown into a pond.[20] Its initial impact is small, but as its ring pattern is repeated on an increasingly greater scale, light and beauty will embrace the entire world.

Korinka is not a set style. It seeks to manifest the artist's spirituality and creativity through the flowers while adhering to the laws of nature. The simplicity of its design speaks of truth that is demonstrated in nature. These arrangements which are patterned after Okada's, remain simple, close to nature. It seems a paradox that the most advanced style is also the most simple in its expression. The philosopher Lao Tsu said, "Simplicity is the highest quality of expression. It is that quality to which art comes in its supreme moments. It makes the final stage of growth. It is the rarest, as it is the most precious result which men secure in their self-training."[21] Instructors of Sangetsu have experienced that it is only through a process that we become one with nature, and

Korinka Arrangement

Figure 3

Korinka Arrangement

Figure 4

can arrange a single flower with skill and reverence.

Why is it that the expression of simplicity in a work of art is viewed as the supreme accomplishment? Okada's response would be that truth is to be found in simplicity, and that nature, in its pure and unadorned state, is truth.[22]

Sangetsu can be said to be a journey to truth; a journey that leads one back to the source. It requires many steps, the first of which is difficult for many students to take. In the western world in particular, the prevailing thought is "more is better"—more flowers, more colors, more stimulation, everything in abundance. It takes time to appreciate arrangements with fewer materials, and a trained eye to see the greater beauty and healing power of simplicity.

Having been a nurse and tended to those who were ill, and also having experienced illness myself, I believe this aspect of simplicity is especially important in assisting a person's recovery with flowers. An individual suffering from illness is already overwhelmed by the inner turmoil in his soul and the outer circumstances which may have contributed to his condition. A large bouquet of symmetrically arranged flowers, though cheerful, does not, I believe, provide the same healing force. In illness, it is simplicity not abundance that can assist in the healing process.

In 1984, I was required to spend a few weeks on bedrest, followed by several weeks recuperation. I must have known on some level of my being what was about to transpire as I moved into a smaller bedroom, simplifying my space and putting order in my surroundings. I organized, cleaned, and taped a print of Raphael's Sistine

Madonna to my dresser mirror. Two days later I was confined to the room that I had just prepared.

I did not have the energy to read or write, and was left to my thoughts, feelings, and idle staring. A friend who had studied Sangetsu brought me a Korinka arrangement that first week and the weeks to follow. The first was arranged simply with a branch of forsythia, a flower, and some greenery in a small basket. She placed the arrangement on my dresser, and I spent hours appreciating its beauty. The Korinka arrangement brought me solace during those long days. While contemplating its beauty, I could smile, be grateful, and calm my thoughts and emotions.

Two years later I experienced illness from the perspective of a family member watching someone you love suffer. Although I had worked in intensive care, its significance took on greater dimensions when my father was a patient in that unit following surgery. The experience tapped a level of emotion I had not previously encountered, leaving me scarred, exhausted, and with the screaming awareness of our vulnerability.

I made a Korinka arrangement using a branch of curly willow and a protea, with a few delicate mums and greens, and took it to the hospital. As there was no room for its placement by my father's bedside, I was asked to display it at the nurses' station in the center of the unit. The arrangement was received with great enthusiasm, and the nurses commented that they had never seen anything like it. It was difficult for me to watch my father's suffering, and I turned to the flower arrangement to give me peace and strength when I felt I had none. I do not know if he noticed the arrangement on the counter those first few days, but I do know that it gave life and energy to the room and to those of us who were in its circle of light.

More recently, I visited a friend in the coronary care unit at a hospital in Santa Monica and gave her an arrangement I had made using a small white calla lily, a yellow freesia, and a piece of sword fern in a black ceramic vase. It provided her with something refreshing and beautiful to focus on for the duration of her hospital stay. Later, she told me that everyone who had entered her room—doctors, nurses, housekeeping, etc.—commented on the arrangement. They were amazed that anything so simple could be so beautiful.

A Korinka arrangement is a powerful symbol of healing. It embraces the spiritual energies of fire, water, and earth, emitting a healing energy that ensouls the environment, and affects people. When a person is ill, he is no longer in his true state of being. A Korinka arrangement symbolizes the perfection and balance in the universe (macrocosm) and in the human being (microcosm). In its beauty, it can reflect a picture of true health for the person at a time when he is unable to do so himself. By viewing these life-filled flowers, an impulse for healing is given.

Ikebana means "flowers which have life," but as Okada pointed out, not all arrangements are an Ikebana— not all arrangements are a display of life-filled flowers. There are those whose arrangements neither retain their vitality nor express the truth of nature. These are not arrangements that can inspire or assist in the healing process.

Korinka Arrangement

Figure 5

Korinka Arrangement

Figure 6

The elements of fire, water, and earth give us life and sustain it. They are most visible at work in nature, and can, therefore, be brought into consciousness through teaching Sangetsu. People need to be reawakened to their relationship to nature—to the planet, to the animals, and to their fellow humans. This requires an inner transformation that is possible when arranging plant materials that carry within their physical form these universal energies. Kado Sangetsu-Ryu, the way of Sangetsu school, is a way back— to nature, to truth, to self, to God.

*In surveying the whole evolution:*
*plant, animal, man, one discovers*
*definite relationship between them.*

*Rudolf Steiner*


*Chapter Three*


## The Living Earth:  Plants, Humankind, Healing

The earth provides the setting in which the physical cycle of life manifests and flourishes.  We establish homes upon its surface, grow food in its soil, and appreciate its abundant processes.  All kingdoms of life are nurtured by this great Mother which would not be possible if she were not also alive.

Leonardo Da Vinci creates a picture of the living earth in his statement, "The earth has a spirit of growth, its flesh is the soil, its bones the stratification of the rock which forms the mountains, its blood the springs of water, the increase and decrease in the blood is represented in the ebb and flow of the sea."[1]

While people experience the earth as their habitat, not all have considered it to be a self-conscious being with a life force of its own, one which breathes and ages as does humankind.  In 1827, Johann Wolfgang von

33

Goethe stated in a conversation with his secretary, "I compare the earth and her atmosphere to a great living being perpetually inhaling and exhaling."[2] As previously mentioned, Okada also spoke of the earth as a living being which breathes once a year; exhaling during spring and summer; inhaling during fall and winter.

As we live in the earth's embrace, her activities have impact in the lower kingdoms of nature and in the higher kingdom of humankind. The earth's breathing, for example, is believed by some to influence the inner and outer rhythms of the human being. Rudolf Steiner has stated, "...What runs its course in one year in the earth takes place quickly eighteen times in one minute in man."[3] Steiner also equates the inner rhythm of four pulse beats to one breath in the human being to what we experience outwardly in nature and the universe: spring is one pulse beat; summer the second pulse beat; fall the third pulse beat; and on the fourth pulse beat, winter, we take a breath.[4]

Outwardly we observe the effects of the earth's breathing on nature, while inwardly we respond to its cycle of expansion and contraction. Our academic school year from September through mid-June is an example of humankind's microcosmic rhythm responding to the greater macrocosm. We commence the school year in the fall as the earth begins to inhale and move into a state of quiet contraction. Those who have not lost their sensitivity to nature, respond to this cycle of inbreathing by being more inwardly focused and able to concentrate. In spring, as the earth begins its exhalation phase and the trees and flowers began to blossom and bear fruit, the human being inwardly experiences the expansion of forces and his energy begins to be directed outward. The cold and darkness of fall and winter moves into the light and warmth of spring and summer. We culminate the school year near the peak of the earth's exhalation when it would be most difficult to remain focused on academic studies. The current trend toward year-round school, I believe, indicates a loss of the oneness of nature and the human being that was once prevalent. Okada believed that it is humankind's deviation from nature, from truth, that has caused its problems, and that we must return to following her example in order to live in harmony with the earth and each other.

There are many relationships that exist between the earth and the kingdoms she nurtures that teaches this harmony. Steiner offers a description of a three-part system that exists equally in humankind and nature as a means of elucidating the unity in all life. The three systems are characterized as the nerve-sense system, the metabolic-limb system, and the rhythmic system. In the structure of the human being the nerve-sense system is primarily the head.[5] The rhythmic component encompasses the lungs and heart or breathing and circulation.[6] The metabolic-limb system includes organs of digestion, reproduction, and the four limbs.[7] These are not to be construed as functioning solely within the body area mentioned, as all three systems extend throughout the human organism. They do, however, have a primary focus in the area described.

In Steiner's philosophy the head is the object of the nerve-sense system. It houses the brain and other sense organs through which we perceive the world. The human head is spherical in shape, its outer covering is hard to the touch, and the symmetrical halves of the face mirror each other as does the brain. These organs remain at rest and are basically immobile in the head. This region of the body remains at a cooler temperature in relation to the other areas as a requisite to its functioning. The necessity of this is demonstrated when a person has a fever or becomes emotionally overheated in his head. We have sayings in our culture which express this imbalance such as, "he's lost his cool," or "he's a hot head," otherwise intimating that the person has ceased to function in a logical or healthy manner.

Another important characteristic is that brain cells only multiply until the age of eighteen months and do not regenerate during the course of the human being's life.[8] These cells then die at a rate of 50-100 per minute.[9] As we use our senses to be conscious during the day, we become fatigued and cannot continue to function without rest. Steiner indicates that to be awake in our senses causes a breaking down process in our physical body. This process includes a gradual mineralization or hardening of the human organism which is a characteristic of the nerve sense-system.[10] According to Steiner, this area of our organism is identified with the function of "thinking."

The metabolic-limb system functions at the opposite pole of the human being. Whereas the nerve-sense system is associated with a breaking down process or death, the metabolic system is concerned with the building up processes or life. The mucosa of the intestinal tract renews itself every five to seven days.[11] Regeneration of the liver is possible, unlike the brain, and our species is propagated through the reproductive organs. The metabolic system contains soft tissues; there is movement, life, and warmth. Warmth is vital to movement and the processes of life whereas cold is more appropriately linked to the functions of immobility and breaking down. Due to the activity of our metabolic system as well as our limbs, this pole of our body is associated with the aspect of "will."

The polarity of the upper and lower processes can be seen in the hard covering and symmetrical mirroring of the organs of the head as opposed to the soft, asymmetry of the metabolic system. One seeming contradiction, however, is to be found in the symmetry of the kidneys and gonads which belong to the metabolic system. Embryology teaches that these organs originate in the head organization of the embryo and only later drop down into the abdomen, preserving in the process the same symmetry as found in the head.[12] Thus are the similarities to be found between the two poles. A thought is conceived in the head. The delicate brain is cushioned from shocks by the cerebrospinal fluid. As a parallel, a human life is conceived in the reproductive organs which is then cushioned from shocks in a sac of amniotic fluid.[13]

The nerve-sense system and the metabolic-limb system meet in the rhythmic system, in the breathing and blood circulation. This system has characteristics of both the upper and lower poles as can be seen by the hard thoracic cage which protects the softer organs of the heart and lungs. This system which stands in the middle, serves to balance and harmonize the two poles. "It is the function of the rhythmical system to ensure that neither the building process of metabolism, nor the breaking down process of the nervous system gains the upper hand, as this must result in illness."[14] The rhythmic system is the realm of "feeling."

Demonstrating the unity that exists between humankind and the earth, Gerbert Grohmann in *The Plant*, applies this threefold distinction to geography. "The outer appearance of the plant world itself shows us that the metabolic system of the earth organism is in the tropics, the head system at the poles, and that the temperate zones correspond to the rhythmic system in man."[15]

At the polar regions of the earth the sun rises once a year and sets half a year later. The water remains frozen for the majority of the year, and the region is characterized by its cold and mineralizing forces. The poles do not absorb the light and warmth which results in plants that are dwarfed and hardened.

The metabolic system of the earth is to be found in the tropics where growth is abundant due to the absorbed heat, light, and rain. Colorful plants and fragrant vegetation thrive in this environment. The temperate regions of the earth are analogous to the rhythmic system producing those plants which tend neither to one extreme or the other. Just as the three systems in the human being can be seen in each area of the body, "Every mountain repeats in miniature what the earth as a prototype is as a whole...The metamorphosis of the vegetation from the high mountains to the lowlands is comparable to that from pole to equator."[16]

Steiner has described plants as the hairs on the head of the earth. This is a wonderful visualization for understanding their relationship to the earth and to its geography. All plant life seems to grow harmoniously within its setting, like the cactus in the desert. I have observed that the color of the soil is often reflected in the natural growth which springs from it, or is perfectly complementary to it. Just as we have blondes, brunettes, and redheads in the human family, varied are the forms and colors of the plants as the hairs on the head of the earth. Forces within and without the earth find expression in the plant. Whether it be the tundra of the poles or the lush plants of the tropics, each is in perfect harmony with its environment and has its unique beauty. Such is the perfection of Great Nature.

Extending the three-part distinction to the plant, we find an intriguing mirror-image reversal in that the plant can be viewed as man upside down.[17] Steiner views the root as analogous to the nerve-sense system of the human being. After its initial stage of growth which thrives with life, it is subject to the earth's mineralization and gradually hardens. The root perceives its environment in the soil, extending its tips into the darkness, and often appears to be similar to the color of the grey matter of the brain. The plant grows from its root upwards, sensing the direction of gravity through starch granules contained in the root tips. The plant appears to have a sense of balance in relation to gravity, so that any imbalance causes it distress.[18]

Similarly, the human being develops from its head downward—the head generally being the largest part of the body at birth. An interesting analogy is also made by Steiner between the starch granules role in maintaining balance in the plant to the otoliths in the human ear.[19] These minute particles are located within the semicircular canals of the ear which are responsible for a person's maintaining balance and posture, the disturbance of which can cause distress.

Steiner's spiritual science explains that the plant sends down its root into the soil and thus unites with the earth and all other plants. The human being, on the other hand, stands with his root, his head, in the spirit which is directed toward the heavens, thus uniting him with his source and other spiritual beings.

The root of the plant stands in relation to the human head; the blossom to the metabolic system. The digestive portion of the plant and the organs that assist in reproduction are to be found in the blossom, with warmth as the essential element for its functions. The budding flower receives the heat of the sun which makes it possible to bloom and to form seed. The blossom receives its nutritive substance from the plant portion, which it then digests and transforms.[20] Those organs which assist in the reproduction of the plant, the stamens and stigma, are contained in this portion of the plant just as the human gonads are also located in the metabolic system.

The leaf mediates between the root and blossom, and is referred to as the "lung of the plant."[21] It corresponds to the rhythmic system in the human being which mediates between the nerve-sense and metabolic systems. The human being inhales oxygen and exhales carbon dioxide. The plant, on the other hand, assimilates the carbon dioxide and releases oxygen. Through photosynthesis, a process that requires light, the plant takes in carbon dioxide from the air and water from the soil, making carbohydrates and releasing the by-product of oxygen. A balance between the kingdoms of nature is therefore maintained. A similar polarity can be seen between the green chlorophyll of the plant and the red hemoglobin in the human being.[22]

Grohmann explains that the plant does not have an individual rhythm such as the pulse rate and breathing ratio found in the human rhythmic system. Instead, its rhythm is determined by the earth's rhythm of seasons and growth since it is joined to it through root and soil.[23]

As previously mentioned, the plant can be viewed as man upside down. This upside down relationship between the plant and the human being also serves as a basis for the healing science of homeopathy. An individual experiencing an illness primarily in the nerve-sense system might be given a natural remedy prepared from the root of the plant; a metabolic-limb system imbalance would be treated with the blossom or seed; and the leaf will affect conditions of the rhythmic system.[24] This is another example of the harmony between the plant and human kingdoms.

Nature's intent is to demonstrate the oneness of all life, be it in the mineral, the plant, the animal, the human being, or in the greater macrocosm. A single flower also expresses this unity. Through its placement in an arrangement we develop an inner awareness that brings us closer to all the earth's kingdoms, and assists us in finding our own center of being. This is possible not only due to the power of nature and its forces which are present in the plant materials, but by making a Sangetsu arrangement the nerve-sense, rhythmic, and metabolic-limb systems and their corresponding soul faculties of thinking, feeling, and willing—the whole human being— are simultaneously engaged in the creation process.

Expressing nature's virtue in an arrangement requires a certain amount of skill and technique. We engage the nerve-sense system when we observe with our senses. Our thought processes become more alert and are strengthened through our attention to detail. We must ascertain the direction, line, and rhythm of our materials in order to display them to their best advantage. We must use our cognitive faculties to utilize space and composition correctly, and to coordinate the harmony between flowers and vase, and placement in the

41

room. In short, we must think about what we are going to do. Our thoughts while arranging also have an effect on the artistic result and the healing energy that is emitted once the arrangement is complete.

Our feelings are also very much involved in making an arrangement. To become "one with the flower" and to receive its inspiration we must approach it with an attitude of gratitude, reverence, and devotion. How does the flower wish to be arranged? How can I best express its unique qualities? What message does it bring to my heart? Not only does this frame of mind put us in touch with nature, but in the process it purifies our thoughts and feelings and gradually refines our character. I have also experienced a corresponding physical response in breathing more deeply and the pulse rate slowing in synchronization, and having a sense of well-being throughout the body. Through the mediating quality of the rhythmic system, balance is achieved in the human organism.

As we begin to feel our materials, our thoughts are quieted and we arrange in an active but meditative state. With our hands we touch the stems and sense the texture and quality of each of our materials. In the realm of doing as in the realm of thought and feeling, gratitude, reverence, and devotion must guide our hands. Do we handle our flowers in a way that enables them to retain their life forces? Does the gentleness of our touch express gratitude for their sacrifice and service? Are we skillful and arrange them swiftly and with determination to create a picture that expresses their greatest beauty? Using our limbs allows us to execute the will of our thoughts and emotions.

We experience the flower first through our senses.

Its color, shape, texture, fragrance, and overall beauty are impressed upon our soul and imbued with feeling. Then we are prompted to act. When making an arrangement, the head (thinking), heart (feeling), and hand (willing) are brought into alignment, a state of being which balances and heals.

> This harmony between the elements of willing, feeling and thinking is such that the inner being of man becomes the substance of Love. This Love is what we may describe as the really creative element in earth existence.[25]

This process of alignment also results in an experience of inner joy and serenity. Alice Bailey writes, "These two qualities of the soul—serenity and joy—are the indications that the soul, the ego, the one who stands alone, is controlling or dominating the personality, circumstance, and all environing conditions of life..."[26] I have experienced these qualities of joy and serenity while arranging flowers. They are not the more transitory emotions of peace or happiness which can be disturbed from one moment to the next. Although some equate happiness with joy and peace with serenity, the experience of these qualities distinguishes their difference—their depth, their enduring quality, the embracing love at their core.

Nature abounds with this love and demonstrates it in the weaving relationships of the earth and the kingdoms in her care. When working with flowers, humankind can vibrate to the same level of love that permeates nature and its kingdoms. A resulting feeling of gratitude will initiate a positive circle of doing good and receiving the same in an individual's life. According to the devas [angels of the plant kingdom], "Gratitude and appreciation have enormous effects, making great swelling movements which complete the circle of life."[27]　By loving mother earth, by revering her gifts through nature, we assist in her growth and continuity, and bring love and healing to ourselves in the process.

*As we see, enjoy*
*The loveliness of all arts,*
*That we are lifted*
*Cleansed in spirit, mind, body,*
*Is one of God's great blessings.*

Mokichi Okada

## Chapter Four

# Transformation

Who am I? Why do I exist? What do my relationships mean? These are burning questions that many seek the answers to during the course of their life.

My first recollection of questioning was at about age five or six. I used to stand in front of my parent's large dresser mirror staring and wondering, "How is it possible that I exist?" "Why am I here in this family and not someone else?" "If I had different parents, would I just look different, or would I not be here at all?" I could not come to terms with the thought that I was a fortuitous event in the life of my parents. "Why me?" I asked again and again; "How is my life possible?" The answers, for me, were not yet to be found.

During the process of growing up and participating more fully in the physical world of responsibilities, I,

45

like most, forgot those questions which once stirred my soul. It was not until my mid-twenties that I had an experience which impacted my life deeply, and which set the hound of heaven upon my heels once again. Finding answers had its price, I was to discover, but there was no turning back. It was an exciting yet painful crossroads, and life for me was forever changed. What is the being of humankind? I had to know. I had to experience.

As a nurse, I was schooled in the accepted doctrine of what constitutes a human being. We consist, I learned, of a complex, finite physical body; within the context of the physical body we have a mind and are subject to emotions. It is a reasonable explanation, and one by which I abided for many years, but it doesn't answer the deeper questions of life or death, nor does it explain the ineffable experiences many have while in a physical body. Nor did I find a satisfactory explanation from the numerous churches I had attended. My search continued.

Through one course of study I learned that in 869 A.D., the Ecumenical Council met in Constantinople and altered the previously accepted triune nature of spirit, soul, and body to a duality of but soul and body alone.[1] Progressively, the existence of even a soul has been questioned by philosophers and scientists, creating the chasm we find today between those who believe in a higher self, and those who hold the physical body supreme, believing this one life is all there is.

It was not until 1975 that I was introduced to Mokichi Okada's philosophy, which provided me with an orientation of the human being that started to unravel the mysteries. According to Okada, the human being consists of a physical body which is finite, and a spiritual

46

body which is infinite. The spiritual body occupies the same space as the physical body but is invisible, being of spirit. Following the separation of the spiritual and physical bodies at death, the spiritual body returns to the spiritual realm for a period of purification and maturity before returning once again to the earth plane.

Okada uses the terms "Primary Spirit" and "Secondary Spirit" to further explain the human being. He defines the primary spirit as the soul—the individualized part of God in each person, which enters the ovum through the sperm at the moment of conception.[2] The secondary spirit is what gives each person the drive to accomplish life goals and ambitions, and is also responsible for the negative feelings of anger, jealousy, hatred, and discontent, as well as the impulse to commit evil acts.[3] Okada states that the secondary spirit enters the human being at approximately age two, but can do so earlier or later.[4] Within each individual there is a struggle or soul polishing between doing good (influence of the primary spirit) or evil (stronger secondary spirit influence). The result of this struggle brings us back to our essence which, according to Okada, is spiritual.

> *Even diamonds*
> *Which are so highly treasured,*
> *Would always be dull*
> *Like pebbles, without luster*
> *If they were never polished.[5]*

The primary spirit, although divine in nature, becomes clouded through the individual's negative thoughts, words, and deeds in the present as well as past lives. In other words, darkened areas appear on the spiritual body which was once pure. The intake of foreign substances (medicine, pesticides, environmental pollution, and chemicals) into the body also pollutes the blood stream which, in turn, forms "clouds" on the spiritual body and toxins in the physical body. Clouds are also passed on through the hereditary stream. These clouds solidify layer upon layer. When the spiritual body becomes clouded to a certain degree, the secondary spirit becomes stronger and has greater influence over the individual. A clouded spiritual body also reflects on the physical body and life circumstances as conditions of disease, poverty, and conflict—what Okada refers to as "purifications." Purifications are considered a means of awakening and restoring the individual to his/her true nature.

A third term, "Yukon", is translated as spiritual essence, and is defined by Okada as the spiritual counterpart of the primary spirit or soul which resides in the spiritual realm.[6] The level in the spiritual realm upon which the yukon resides is determined by the purity or cloudiness of the spiritual body. If there are fewer clouds, it ascends to the higher realms of vibration which reflect in the individual's physical life as health, peace and prosperity. If an individual has many clouds, the yukon descends to a lower level of vibration which reflects in misfortune on the physical plane. The position of the yukon changes constantly according to our thoughts, words, and actions. This corresponds to the Doctrine of Karma, or you "reap what you sow"—each person is held accountable.

The primary spirit and yukon are connected by a "Spiritual Cord" which is connected to God (figure 7). As a visualization, the spiritual cord can be likened to an umbilical cord (although invisible) which connects a mother to her child until just after birth. It serves as a conduit so that everything an individuals thinks, says, or does is known immediately on a spiritual level. Also, God's will is conveyed to the individual through this connection.

Each individual forms hundreds, sometimes thousands of spiritual cords with people during his life, and with possessions as well. Some are larger and some are smaller according to the relationship. To emphasize the spiritual cord's importance in human affairs Okada states, "The cord is the conveyer of life-supporting energies, and it influences the fate of human beings and even the world's destiny at large."[7] He also said that the spiritual cord can be broken among friends and acquaintances, but not between blood relatives.[8] Without consciously realizing it, we influence each other for good or ill through our spiritual cords.

The yukon, primary spirit, and secondary spirit can also be thought of in terms of spirit, soul, and body used in other metaphysical works. For simplicity and ease of understanding, Okada generally uses the basic distinction of the spiritual body and the physical body.

A second view of the human being according to spiritual science is offered by Rudolf Steiner. Much of what Okada has imparted through his revelation and spiritual investigation from the East, has been substantiated and further elucidated by Steiner and his direct experience of the spiritual world from the West. Together they present a picture of the human being that rings true for me, and provide a foundation for understanding how flowers can heal and transform.

Rudolf Steiner also identifies the human being as consisting of spirit, soul, and body. "The spirit is immortal; birth and death reign over the body according to the

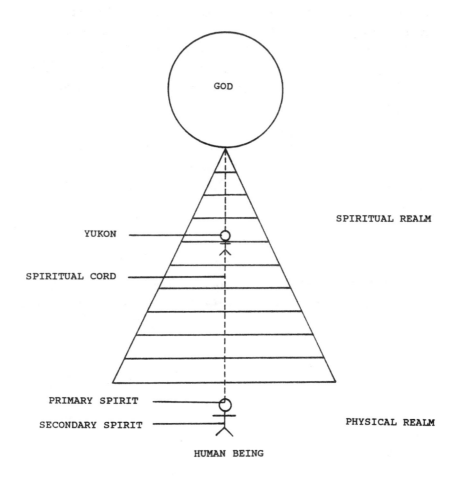

GOD

SPIRITUAL REALM

YUKON

SPIRITUAL CORD

PRIMARY SPIRIT

SECONDARY SPIRIT

PHYSICAL REALM

HUMAN BEING

Figure 7

(Adapted from unpublished introductory course of Johrei Fellowship)

laws of the physical world; the soul life, which is subject to destiny, mediates the connection of both during earthly life."[9]   Steiner conveys this truth in an analogy of a flower: The human being is rooted in the physical world through the body, he comes to flower in the spiritual world through the spirit, and the stalk is the soul that roots in the one and flowers in the other.[10] The physical body acts as a vehicle for the soul, and the soul a vehicle for the spirit, the soul mediating between the eternal and temporal.

To further understand the interaction of the spirit, soul, and body Steiner describes the human being in terms of a physical body, etheric body, astral body and ego.[11]

There is no denial of the "Physical Body." It is tangible and easy to observe with our physical senses, and is our instrument through which we function in everyday life. It is also without dispute that the body is temporary due to its aging process and gradual decline, ultimately resulting in death. Physical science attributes life to the physical bodily processes such as respiration and circulation.   Both Okada and Steiner, however, support the view that the spirit is behind the physical processes which sustain life—the invisible moves the visible. The physical corpse is devoid of any life forces, devoid of spirit, and is subject to a mineralization and decomposition process which returns its elements to the earth.

The last three members of which Steiner speaks are not perceptible to our physical senses as is the physical body. Being of a spiritual essence they must be perceived with spiritual awareness, and are, therefore, not as readily accepted as is the physical body.

The "Etheric Body" is described by Steiner as a supersensible body which gives life and form to the physical organism.[12] For that reason it is also referred to as the body of formative forces. It interpenetrates the physical body and serves as its architect, making a pattern for the physical. All physical organs have their etheric organ counterpart. Even when the physical organ is removed through surgery, the etheric organ, as the spiritual pattern, remains. This is an important point when tending to those who are ill.

The "Astral Body" is the dwelling place of the soul and the vehicle of our sympathies, antipathies, desires, suffering, joy, pain, ideas, and impulses.[13] The soul manifests itself through the activities of thinking, feeling and willing. The feeling or sentient aspect is united with the astral body. We receive impressions from the outside world and process them inwardly. We take these sensations to a higher state of awareness through thought and reflection, and will ourself to act. Through the members of the soul we gain knowledge of the world we live in, and knowledge of our inner self.

The "Ego" or "I" is the uniqueness in each human being. It is due to the presence of the ego that each individual can become a self-conscious and independent being and refer to himself as an "I."[14] No other kingdom on earth can do this. During the course of an individual's life the ego works to transform the astral, etheric, and physical body which then gives birth to higher spiritual levels.

According to Steiner, that the ego is working to transform the astral body can be evidenced by the ennoblement of feelings, and that the individual is no longer at the whim of his emotions. The etheric is the avenue through which the human temperament is expressed, and the working of the ego upon the etheric body manifests as a change in the character or temperament. The ego also works to transform the spiritual forces behind the physical, material body. The ego, says Steiner, is assisted in this process of transformation of the members of the human being by religion and the arts:

> When the "I" allows the impulses that flow from religion to act upon it again and again, they form within it a power that works right into the ether body and transforms it in much the same way that the lesser life-impulses cause a transformation of the astral body. These lesser life-impulses of life, which come to man through study, contemplation, ennobling of the feelings, and so forth, are subject to the manifold changes of existence; religious experiences, however, imprint upon all thinking, feeling, and willing a uniform character...that persists throughout all changes. Religious creed...works by means of constant repetition. It therefore acquires the power of working upon the ether body.

> The influence of true art has a similar effect upon the human being. If through outer form, through color and tone of a work of art, he penetrates to its spiritual basis with thought and feeling, then the impulses that the "I" thus receives work down even into the ether body. If we think this thought through to the end we can estimate what a tremendous significance art has for all human evolution.[15]

Similarly, Okada speaks of transformation of the spiritual in humankind, the changes of which can be observed in the way in which individuals conduct their life. He says that there are three ways to be spiritually purified: 1) through suffering; 2) through the practice of virtue and giving service; and 3) through the appreciation of high-level art and beauty.[16] The easiest way is, of course, through viewing good art. Okada says that without people realizing it their spirit is purified, and their consciousness is raised to higher levels.

Both Steiner and Okada make a distinction in art by saying "true art" and "high-level art," qualifying that not just anything that is called art today can raise humankind's spiritual consciousness.

> *Beware, my people,*
> *For only some works of art*
> *Are heavenly ones,*
> *While some other works of art*
> *Are corrupting, hellish things.*[17]

That not all art is healing, and can, in fact, induce a negative response is corroborated by contemporary transformative artist, Ilana Lilienthal. Lilienthal, whose role as a transformative artist is to change the viewer's consciousness through her paintings, has commented that the creation of violent and negative art appeals to the violent, nervous side of a viewer's character.[18]

Adrian Bernard Klein also writes, "Art is not vital unless it is spiritually powerful enough to unlock the door of heaven. Art is man's witness to the divinity which abides in him...True art is a mystical act, the creation of a sacramental symbol with which to manifest the spirit of truth."[19]

From the above statements we see the importance of the artist's role. Okada indicated that people are not only affected through the art form, be it flower arranging, dance, music, painting, etc., but also by the character and spirituality of the artist. The artist is able to elevate the consciousness of people through his/her art and spiritual being, or to take them to a lower level. For this reason, Okada said that artists have a great responsibility to society, and should be of exceedingly high character. They are then able to play a leading role in transforming human consciousness.

Beyond its mere creation, art has a purpose of transforming the human being. Steiner believed that different art forms expressed the laws at work in each of the four members he described as the physical body, etheric body, astral body, and ego; namely, architecture and the physical body; sculpture and the etheric body; painting and the astral body; music and the ego.[20]

Sangetsu is an expression of a combination of art forms. The asymmetry of form, of line, provides the foundation for the overall harmony of the arrangement. We paint a picture with flowers, each one representing a different stroke of the brush. As we place our materials in the vase, we sculpt the space, taking care to allow for the negative space, or what is called "empty beauty." Thus in making a flower arrangement, we impact the physical body in the architecture of the form; the astral body in the painting of the design; and the etheric body in the sculpting of space. And the ego orchestrates it all.

A Sangetsu arrangement is not only a prototype of the universe, but a symbol of the law of the human being in its seeking to unfold. Through the process of arranging flowers, a combination of forces act to heal and transform the members of the human organism into their higher spiritual natures.

Unable to see the invisible forces at work, most respond to the visible beauty expressed in art and nature. Dorothy Maclean writes, "Beauty is of God....Consciousness of beauty brings you into oneness, into any part of the universe....The more you appreciate beauty, the more you are linked universally."[21] Beauty is not to be thought of as something superfluous to our existence for which we can take time after all else has been attended to. Beauty is as necessary to our soul as food is to our body. It evokes the highest expression in each individual.

An example of its importance is given by Jean Lush, author of *Emotional Phases of a Woman's Life*. Lush relates a story told to her while living in Australia during World War II by a block warden, whose responsibility was to give instruction on air raids, blackouts, and first aid. Once, in reaction to a day he selected for a meeting, the women in the neighborhood responded, "Oh, no! That's the day I buy my flowers. That's my flower arranging day."[22]

> With Japanese submarines in the bay and danger all around them these women wouldn't give up their flower arranging. I'm sure they didn't consciously realize it, but in the midst of trouble, those flowers were basic to their well-being.[23]

Beauty stimulates the soul through the senses, resulting in a feeling of renewal, peace, and, at the same time, enthusiasm (the warm will to act). The feelings of well-being received from appreciating beauty also have a physical-chemical basis as explained by Blair Justice in, *Who Gets Sick*:

> ...when we are moved by music, the beauty of nature or a work of art, we apparently "turn on" and release in the brain opioid substances—endorphins or similar peptides—that give us goose bumps, 'thrills' or other sensations of pleasure.[24]

In Sangetsu it is often said that we arrange the heart of "Shin, Zen, Bi," or "Truth, Virtue, and Beauty." Okada stated:

Heaven is the world of beauty. No matter how conscientious a person may be in his religious pursuits and how good a person he may be, if he lacks interest in the arts, that person is not truly living the life of Shin, Zen, Bi--Truth, Virtue, and Beauty--according to God's will.[25]

The importance of arranging the heart of Shin, Zen, Bi is elucidate by Steiner's philosophy of "Truth, Beauty, and Goodness." He explains how the expression of these ideals enables individuals to realize their full human potentials.

According to Steiner, truth links the human being to his past or pre-earthly existence and is connected with the physical body. The experience of beauty creates a link with the spiritual world in the present earth life and strengthens our reality of the etheric body. Goodness is connected to the astral body, and builds something for the future beyond death.

Steiner indicates that humankind comes into the physical world out of pre-earthly existence, Each receiving a physical body patterned after the spiritual essence which was gathered in the spiritual realm prior to birth. A relationship is thereby established between the truth of our pre-earthly existence and our physical body which is the image. Our feeling for truth, for our past from which we've come, is related to the feeling we have of our physical body. Falsehood severs the spiritual threads, as Steiner describes them, connected with the physical body. "If truth and truthfulness become real experiences, then this means that we are in a certain sense properly lodged in the physical body."[26]

A life without beauty would be a life devoid of spirit. Steiner distinguishes between those who merely

57

look at beauty and those who experience beauty. The experience of beauty will cause a response in the etheric body—a feeling of warmth, illumination, or divinity.[27] To experience beauty is to acknowledge the spiritual world, and to have a right relationship to the etheric body.

To have the desire to do good for the sake of itself, to put the interests of others first, and to be willing to experience the soul of another is what is meant by goodness. Without this aspect of goodness the astral body will not truly be healthy.

> For a man to be true means that he has a right connection with his spiritual past. For a man to have a sense of beauty means that he does not deny in the physical world his connection with the world of the spirit. And for a man to be good means that he nurtures a seed for a spiritual world in the future.[28]

We arrange the heart of truth, virtue, and beauty using greens and flowers. These are not dead substances, but materials alive with spiritual forces. The truth is expressed in the laws of nature that we utilize in our arrangement. Beauty touches us through the flowers, branches, vase, and design we have created. The desire to make others happy and to bring healing to their life fills our heart with goodness, which blesses the flowers and those viewing the arrangement.

According to Steiner, nature abounds with etheric or formative forces similar to what we as humans receive. In other words, the flower, in addition to having its physical body, also has an etheric body. I believe that the etheric life forces of the flower materials assist in the transformation of the etheric body of not only the individual making the arrangement, but that of the viewer as well. We have witnessed changes in character, in temperament, in those studying Sangetsu over a period of time. Steiner teaches that these changes are an indication of a transformation in the etheric body.[29] The spiritual forces at work, the repetition of the guidelines, and the rhythm of class instruction affects the flexible etheric body and brings about change.

It was Okada's vision to place flowers in every prison and jail cell because of the positive effect it would have on the consciousness of the inmates. To this end, Sangetsu has been taught twice a month at the Wakayama Women's Prison in Japan since February 24, 1975, under the direction of Mrs. Hiroko Sakamoto. Mrs. Sakamoto reports that, generally speaking, after about three months the instructors begin to notice a change in the inmates' attitudes. What is more important is that the inmates themselves realize that there has been a change. The following are excerpts from letters written by women inmates on how Sangetsu has helped them:

> I would love to tell you about my mind getting gentle when I arrange flowers. As a result of these two years, I have different dreams than before and wish to create something. Before I came here I never had peaceful feelings, and I was ashamed. My everyday life here is hard with less freedom. I can't wait for the class. Your guidance and teaching have helped me, and I decided not to return here anymore. It was too late to realize the crime I had committed. It was a shame I couldn't control myself. Please guide me more.[30]

A second participant writes:

> Each of the students in the classes is filled with happiness, making mutual comments and suggestions, learning from each others' arrangements. Thinking of my cloudy past and attitudes, I deeply desire once again in my life to be a person having the heart of beauty like flowers.

Another comments:

> While I am watching these flowers, I can forget the sorrow and suffering. Moreover, warm and pleasant feelings well up in my heart. How I wish I could be pure and beautiful like the flowers!

And another:

> I wish to thank you for helping me to learn how to express what I feel in my heart through flower arrangements. By handling the living flowers of the different seasons I become able to convey my deepest feeling onto those beautiful flowers. At such moments I can be free of ego, and my mind becomes clearer, forgetting the fact that I am in prison. The faces of my fellow students in the classroom also are shining with happiness. When I bring back my arrangement to my room and put it on my desk, the atmosphere of the room suddenly becomes brighter and gives the illusion of returning to my real home. The arrangements are always too good to appreciate for just myself, so I take them to the factory and beauty salon to share their beauty. Not only my friends but also customers are very happy to see them. I am so grateful for what I can do with my arrangements. I have learned that how my heart and mind are reflects on my arrangements. The flowers seem to constantly talk to me so that I feel easier to understand their heart. It is so enjoyable to make conversation with flowers. I would like to discipline myself to grow spiritually to be sweet and gracious like those flowers.

We have also had many reports of changes in temperament of those in the area of the arrangement's placement. It has been my experience and others that the energy of the flowers permeates the environment, changing the vibrations and atmosphere. The space comes to life, and when individuals look at the flowers, they are permeated with these life forces and the harmony in the atmosphere that has been created by them. This has given rise to the placement of Sangetsu arrangements in mayor's offices, police stations, schools, prisons, and other businesses. There are always responses to the arrangement, and it is noticed when one is not there.

In addition to teaching classes for the inmates at Wakayama Women's Prison, the instructors also made an arrangement for the prison officers. Initially, the officers were difficult. After a time, Mrs. Sakemota reports that they changed their attitude and began to treat the instructors with kindness and appreciation. They had experienced that having a flower arrangement in their presence made them less nervous and more peaceful.[31] The officers are transferred every two years, and now they ask the Sangetsu instructors to arrange flowers for their new offices as well.

One of my students makes an arrangement for her bookstore each week and enjoys the response it brings from her customers. She has commented that some customers are quite boisterous upon entering the store, but then see the flower arrangement and immediately become quiet. Others peer around the corner and go seeking for a second arrangement in the hallway. Each visitor has a comment to make about the flowers.

We become aware of a transformation in the astral body through increased sense perception, response to color, and ennoblement of the feelings, all of which reflect in the individual's attitude toward the flowers, and in expression of feelings in one's life. I asked Sangetsu students to comment on their experience of arranging flowers, and changes they had noticed to which they replied:

61

Making a flower arrangement is like meditating. It brings peace and calmness and a forgetting of all else. The appreciation of the beauty of the flowers carries over into other areas of my life. By noticing colors and line I look at my garden and notice the way nature has combined the flowers and the leaves. My home feels different when I have flowers in it. I feel different—I think I feel more at one with my environment.[32]

## Another comments:

I have found that it increases my awareness and appreciation of nature, and that this can also transfer to my awareness and appreciation of life. No matter what frame of mind or state of being I am in at the start of class, I find that there is always a shift within myself—a positive one. Stress and tensions of the day are released and I am much more relaxed. I can also say that I am in a more loving state of being. Having the flower arrangement in my home is an added benefit. It helps me to focus my attention so that as I look at it, whatever stress is on my mind it is released. The beauty of the flowers is calming and centering. People coming into my home notice the flower arrangement and comment in a positive way. As I am out and about in the world I am more aware of flowers, plants, and bushes. Noticing how they grow, their relationship to other things around them, and again that quiet inner quality that comes from them are all areas that I am more aware and appreciative of in my life.

## Another student writes:

Making the Sangetsu arrangements give me a peaceful feeling, a sort of tranquility within me. I like myself after I finish. I always look forward to classes, and so do the men at the office because they know that I'll be bringing fresh flowers for a new arrangement.

And another:

> I sometimes go to class feeling distracted or anxious about something in my day, but after working with the flowers and focusing on the creation of beauty, I feel renewed. As I have been studying Sangetsu many years, I often do arrangements outside of class using the materials of my own garden. This is most satisfying and provides a continuity and connection between my gardening and flower arranging interests. It has also made me realize that at any time of year there is always something in the yard worth enjoying and appreciating. Often the most humble materials will make the most interesting arrangements. I have always been an artist, and constantly deal with questions of line, composition, color, rhythm, and expression. Sangetsu helps me to further refine these sensibilities.

> An interest in nature and the details of nature have always been an aspect of my art. I frequently am inspired to clean and straighten the areas around the arrangement in ever widening circles to extend that sense of harmony. I constantly receive compliments from friends and business associates who visit our home and express surprise and delight at the beauty that can be expressed by a few simple branches and flowers.

How are these transformations possible? According to Okada, the flower arrangement purifies the spiritual body of spiritual clouds which refines the secondary nature and elevates the spiritual being. This allows the essence of the human being to quietly and effortlessly come into its own. The flowers also purify the spiritual atmosphere which interpenetrates our physical space, dispelling the collective spiritual clouds and negative vibrations sent forth by peoples in a particular area. Flowers change the environment with the result that people feel refreshed, uplifted, and joyful. Serenity also fills the space.

This follows what Okada calls one of the basic laws of the universe—the "Law of the Spiritual Preceding the Physical." This law states that everything first occurs on a spiritual level and is then reflected into the physical.[33] Illness is a case in point..."illness is essentially an effect, the cause of which lies in the spiritual body. Clouds appear on one or several areas of the spiritual body, and these clouds reflect on the physical body as an illness. When the clouds are eliminated, illness must disappear."[34] Steiner concurs that illness arises in the spiritual members of the human being and works its way down into the physical body. The treatment of only physical symptoms, therefore, merely suppresses the condition. Healing of the physical body does not occur until the spirit is healed. This is a reason why art therapy is important for those who are ill. "...whenever the doctor employs an artistic activity for the purpose of healing, he calls upon productive powers which are latent in everyone...[which are then] absorbed and transformed into positive qualities."[35]

The arts heal on a spiritual level which can then reflect in the physical organism. Flowers, in particular, work on the soul and the etheric body. By making Sangetsu arrangements or viewing them when ill, it is possible to purify these spiritual members and establish a new pattern of health in the etheric, which will then reflect in the physical body.

Sangetsu is more than an art form. It is an instrument through which we can be transformed in spirit, soul, and body, thus creating a new prototype of living in harmony with ourself and our world.

## Chart of Relationships

| | | | | | | |
|---|---|---|---|---|---|---|
| ○ | Oneness | Spirit | Yukon | Fire | Sun | Father | Blossom |
| △ | Duality | Soul | Primary Spirit | Water | Moon | Mother | Leaf |
| □ | Manifestation | Body | Secondary Spirit | Soil | Earth | Child | Root |

Figure 8

*He to whom nature begins to
unveil her open secrets, feels
an irrestistible longing for her
worthiest interpreter, art.*

*Goethe*

# Chapter Five

## Metamorphosis of Plants and Human Life Cycles

Johann Wolfgang von Goethe (1749-1832) is remembered by most for his literary genius. His interests and contribution to human understanding, however, far exceeded poetry extending into the scientific fields as well. His botanical studies and theory of colors continue to serve as a legacy to the unity of all life.

Nature was a source of wonder and joy for Goethe, and he regarded this teacher in the highest esteem. Through his devoted study, Goethe introduced a new way of viewing nature apart from his predecessors. While Karl Linnaeus, Swedish botanist (1707-1778), categorized plants based upon their external form and structure, Goethe's investigation concerned their inner nature. "What he [Linne] sought to separate by force, I, in accordance with the inner needs of my being, had to strive with all my might to unite."[1] What is the common element whereby a plant becomes a plant and not something else? This was a question that gave impetus to Goethe's quest to understand nature from the inside out, and from the whole to the part.

It was Goethe's view that the thing in itself, be it a plant or other, reveals its mystery through correct observation and attitude of soul. He experienced this phenomenon in Strassburg while contemplating a cathedral tower from a room in which he was staying. In *Goethe and the Art of Healing,* Friedrich Husemann relates the story that when a member of Goethe's party commented on the cathedral's unfortunate state of incompleteness having only one tower, Goethe remarked that it was equally unfortunate that the tower itself had not been complete and proceeded to describe its appearance as it should have been.[2] A gentleman, who had the cathedral's plans in his keeping, overheard Goethe's conversation and his accurate description of the original intent, and asked who had told him this information. Goethe replied, "The tower itself. I have looked at it so long and have bestowed upon it so much affection that it finally decided to reveal to me this open secret."[3]

Goethe's investigation into the being of nature took him on a journey to Italy where, in 1787, he discovered what he called the "Urpflanze" or archetypal plant. "Each of her [nature's] works has an essential nature of its own, each of her manifestations a most isolated concept; and yet all comprises only one."[4] The archetypal plant for Goethe was the "Idea" or the principle that remains constant through the varied manifestations and fluctuating movements in the process of its becoming. Rudolf Steiner, who edited Goethe's works, provided this description of the urpflanze:

The totality of formative principles which organize the plant, making it what it is, and whereby we are able to think of a particular object of Nature and say: 'this is a plant'—this totality is the archetypal plant, the Urpflanze. As such, it is an Idea to be grasped only in the ideal world of thought. It acquires a definite form, size, colour, organic plurality, etc. This outward form is not fixed, but is subject to endless variations, all in keeping with the same Idea or totality of formative laws, and resulting from it necessarily. Having once grasped these structural principles, these typical requirements—the archetypal forces of the plant—one has the key to every individual plant in Nature.[5]

Experiencing the urpflanze was not an end for Goethe, but a beginning. He wanted to know how the formative forces of the archetype work into the growth of the plants. Through his constant observation, drawing of the plants and taking them into his being, he was led to discover the metamorphosis of plants—"The process by which one and the same organ presents itself to us in manifold forms."[6] Goethe observed that growth occurs from seed to fruit or flower and back to seed again in alternating cycles of expansion and contraction. These steps are elucidated by Steiner in his introduction to Goethe's scientific works:

In the seed the plant formation is most intensely contracted. With the forming of leaves, there follows the first unfolding expansion of the formative forces. What is pressed together to a point in the seed becomes spatially expanded in the leaves. In the calyx, the forces are again concentrated around an axial point. The corolla is produced by the next expansion. Stamens and pistils come about from the next concentration, the fruit through the last (third) expansion, whereupon the total force of the plant life conceals itself again in the seed.[7]

Goethe discovered that each organ of the plant is a metamorphosis of the leaf. This is a fascinating phenomenon. I have observed metamorphosis in the lily of the nile and the calla lily, and, on occasion, have made arrangements with tulips and irises whose petals were in the process of changing from leaf to flower. Students, too, are filled with wonder when I am able to show them flowers whose metamorphosis from leaf to blossom is not yet complete.

Goethe concludes, "Whether then the plant vegetates, blossoms, or bears fruit, it nevertheless is always the same organs, with varying function and with frequent changes in form, that fulfill the dictates of Nature."[8]

The dynamic of plant growth springs forth from the germ seed, but is nurtured into life and form through the sun, water, and soil, and with the assistance of nature spirits otherwise known as elementals or fairies. According to Steiner, there are four groups of nature spirits that tend to plant growth: Gnomes (root-spirits), Undines (water-spirits), Sylphs (air-spirits), and Salamanders (fire-spirits).[9]

The first stage of plant growth beneath the earth's surface is cared for by the gnomes. The gnomes live in the earth and busy themselves around the root of the plant. They have the tasks of bringing the earth's mineral substance to the root, and of pushing the plant out of the earth.[10] That the plant rises vertically, breaking through the earth's surface is due to the work of the gnomes. Gnomes are portrayed in folklore as having a rather old face, a pointed beard, and wearing a pointed hat. Dora van Gelder, who had fairies for playmates and the higher perception to see and communicate with them verifies this characterization in her book, *The Real World of Fairies*. "They have old faces and little beady black eyes...the long jaw gives the effect of a pointed beard. The wooly material which covers the head also rises into a point, so the whole head gives the effect of a double triangle."[11]

Once the shoot is pushed above ground and the leaves make their appearance, the undines begin their work. Steiner calls these water-spirits the "chemists of plant-life" as they unite and disperse substances necessary to the growth and formation of the plant.[12] As the gnomes are connected to the earth and what is earthly, the undines are at home in the etheric element of water and moisture. Their form is not as defined as the gnomes, preferring to be in a state of constant transformation.

The sylphs find their well-being in the airy-warmth element and have a special relationship to birds in whose air currents they love to move. The task of the sylphs is to bring light into the plant and to mold this light, along with what has been provided by the undines, into the archetypal form. The gnomes then receive this ideal image through the plant down into the earth where it will later contribute to the process of fructification.

The fire-spirits or salamanders assist the plant by bringing warmth into the blossom where it is concentrated in the seed. They feel akin to the insect world, and rely upon their flight from one flower to the next in order to distribute warmth to the seedbuds.

> Everywhere they follow in the tracks of the insects as they buzz from blossom to blossom. And so one really has the feeling, when following the flight of insects, that each of these insects as it buzzes from blossom to blossom, has a quite special aura which cannot be entirely explained from the insect itself...It is because it is accompanied by a fire-spirit...[13]

It is generally believed that reproduction in the plant takes place in the organs within the blossom. Steiner, however, indicates from a spiritual point of view, that fructification occurs through the activity of the salamanders and the gnomes—the fire-spirits utilizing the stamens, pollen, and anthers to carry the warmth to the seed vessel, which then goes into the earth womb to unite with the ideal plant form preserved by the gnomes.[14] And thus the process begins again.

I attended a lecture several years ago at which I learned that each of these nature spirits bears a message for humankind: "The gnomes, who have universal knowledge, want us to 'wake up'; the undines cannot understand that we are the same and say, 'change more, be flexible'; the sylphs remind us of our creativity—'be creative' is their message; and the salamanders, 'take responsibility for the future.' In the warmth of our will we have a task for the future—realize your possibilities."[15]

Having become well acquainted with fairies on her father's plantation in Java, Dora van Gelder paints a more whimsical picture of the typical garden fairy. "I talked to them by making a very strong mental picture. Sometimes they would tap me on the hand or forehead, just as a leaf touches me in falling; that is when they wanted me to play with them, or to look at their flower or bush."[16]

According to van Gelder, garden fairies express tremendous joy in living. They are both curious and playful and are akin to youth in the plant, animal, or human. They especially like babies who are, as they are, spontaneous and happy. Each one has a plant or plants in their care to which they give great attention. "They show their feelings in action, and they often stay with one flower quite a while, just as though it were their baby, petting and loving it..."[17] Fairies are in constant motion, and may not necessarily stay in one garden. They watch people with a modicum of interest, preferring babies and children, but more are attracted to those humans who tend lovingly to their garden, and perhaps understand that fairies do exist.

When we plant flowers in our garden and watch them spring from seed to blossom, we attribute their growth solely to the sunlight, to adequate water, and to the nutrients in the soil. But, as Steiner and van Gelder have pointed out, the invisible helpers are behind the visible process—the spiritual interweaves with the physical. My students have often commented how they think about the little beings in their yard once I have spoken of their role in nature. Visualizing the variety of fairies of the earth, water, air, and fire elements that assist in the growth and care of the plants in our gardens, brings a feeling to our heart that deepens our appreciation and love for nature. When we begin to understand the love and joy in which nature is grown and how it arrives in its great beauty, we cannot help but to want to further glorify it in a flower arrangement, expressing its inward life and outward appearance.

The wonder that exists in the metamorphosis and growth of plants is also demonstrated in the cycles of human life. As Mother Earth provides the womb in which to nurture the seed that will become a plant, a fertilized ovum finds its nurturing in the womb of its human mother. The obvious physical vehicle and care contribute to the life of this new being; the spiritual forces, however, stand behind and guide its growth and development. According to Steiner's spiritual science, the spirit-germ and physical-germ unite at conception, but it is not until three or four weeks later that the ego, astral, and etheric members take hold of what has been created by the spirit-germ and physical-germ.[18] Each of the higher members becomes more active at varying intervals during the nine month period of gestation. "Something unites with the germ of the human being which is not derived from mother or father and yet belongs to him."[19]

Dr. Michel Odent describes the process of birth as asymmetric. "It's common to see women search for an asymmetrical position of the pelvis, going through the birth canal is an asymmetric process."[20] As the flower is pushed up out of the ground in a single stalk, so does the infant emerge from the womb through an asymmetric birth canal. Everywhere in nature we find asymmetry. We use this principle in making a Sangetsu arrangement because it is asymmetry which brings harmony and life to the arrangement.

The plant moves from leaf to leaf and then to flower and/or fruit. In a similar fashion the human being evolves through different stages of consciousness and physical form as he blossoms into his being. Steiner has characterized the growth of the human being in seven year cycles, each cycle having a particular purpose in spiritual and physical development. That there is appropriate learning which corresponds to development at each stage caused Steiner, in 1919, to initiate a course of education based upon nature and the rhythm of the human being.* To force a bud to prematurely open and expose its blossom is not in accord with the laws of nature which fulfill the patterns of growth. Following nature's example, it is also not healthy for the child to be forced into growth and learning prior to its time. We must allow him to unfold according to the inner laws of being.

Metamorphosis in the human being can be seen from one cycle to the next as an intensification or change. Also, what transpires in one phase of life will reflect in a later period. "It becomes manifest in the observation of a life that the real effect of what was introduced as causes into the childish soul appear only at the very latest—that in the evening of life."[21] This regards both qualities of the soul and conditions of the physical body, each having an effect upon the other. One example of soul metamorphosis indicated by Steiner is that reverence and devotion developed in childhood become in later life the power to bless.[22]

The human life unfolds rhythmically if not obstructed by outside circumstances, much the same as nature thrives due to the order that prevails. We also have a rhythm in our Sangetsu curriculum directed at leading the student to an increased level of awareness regarding nature and life while developing artistic skills.

I view this process as three spirals: one moving from the periphery to the center; one moving from the center to the periphery; and one moving upward but circling back around before going to the next higher level. Through our instruction we gradually lead the student from the western consciousness of abundance and sym metry (from the periphery to the center), to the eastern concept of simplicity, asymmetry, and line. This is also

* Waldorf education provides a balanced curriculum in the arts and sciences according to the growing rhythm of the child.

the direction of becoming one with nature and becoming centered in the self. The simultaneous movement from the center to the periphery has to do with the expansion of consciousness that should parallel the act of arranging flowers. As the student moves back out into the world, he or she should begin to see the unity of all life. It is also going from one's center and reaching out in an ever expanding circle to family, friends, and community.

The third spiral has to do with the method of teaching. We begin the upward movement by teaching basic arrangements to develop the artistic eye, and to become familiar with the skills required to complete an arrangement. We then teach more creative styles that break away from the basic forms while maintaining the guidelines. Next, we circle back briefly (in the first few courses) to review styles and technique. The principles are learned through this process of repetition which will work into the etheric body and carry the memory of those guidelines and how to utilize them. The ability to be creative and to accurately express nature is the goal of this spiral. Success will depend upon the student's participation and interest in this step by step process.

> *The basic reason*
> *Great Nature constantly thrives-*
> *Improves and expands-*
> *Is that each and every part moves*
> *Along in perfect order.*[23]

The Sangetsu school is patterned after nature. The spiritual and physical unfolding of the human being also follows a natural order. I have found that the styles we teach can also parallel the unfolding consciousness that characterize a particular time in a human being's life. For example, a young child's world is relatively simple. The journey of his life is just beginning, and what he will someday express is only there in potential. To indicate this stage a Korinka arrangement could be made using a single rose in an appropriate container, and delight as it gradually opens into the beautiful flower it is ( figure 9).

In the primary grade years we meet a plethora of new experiences and challenges, and are called upon to use the function of our right and left brain. Correspondingly, we have a right floral figure and a left floral figure.* (refer to figure 1) It is of interest that just as some people are more right-brain artistic or left-brain analytic, students, as a rule, will have more difficulty arranging to one side or the other, the left floral figure presenting the greatest challenge.

The world through the eyes of a teenager is more expansive and opinionated than prior to puberty. Steiner refers to the first year of high school as a time when things take on a perspective of polarity—they are either black or white. In Sangetsu we have a polarity arrangement called plane and mass, which consists of two opposites blended together to create harmony ( figure 10).

The upper grades are a time of greater activity and awareness. Our rhythmical line arrangements, such as lively motion (figure 11) and parallel lines (figure 12), express this movement and expansion. Two arrangements come to mind when I think of a student graduating. One, is a large arrangement that symbolizes all the

* In a right floral arrangement the earth line points in the direction of the right shoulder but is arranged on the left side of the vase. The left floral figure is arranged on the right side of the vase.

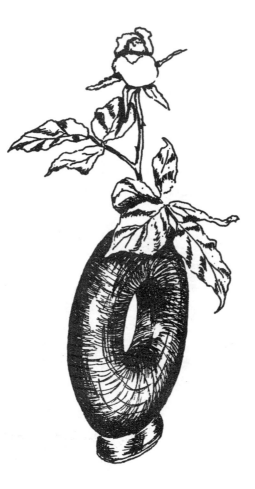

Korinka Arrangement
Figure 9

Plane And Mass
Figure 10

Lively Motion
Figure 11

Parallel Lines
Figure 12

experiences and changes in consciousness that his journey has led him through. The other, once again, is a rose for it holds in its simplicity all experience and yet signifies the beginning of another cycle of potential development (figures 13 & 14).

The flowers continue to speak throughout the cycles of life and life's circumstances. One arrangement, for example, addresses the fact that it is common in our culture to have a household headed by only one parent. Sangetsu's omission arrangement, which omits one main line, demonstrates how balance and harmony can still be maintained in this new configuration among the family of flowers (See figure 15).

Our Sangetsu arrangements can speak of many things—cycles of life, circumstances of life, the seasons, celebrations, and emotions because they represent life itself, and serve as an inspiration and pattern for humankind to follow. It is said that within each of us lies a perfect flower waiting to unfold. Life's experiences provide the opportunity, and nature shows us the way.

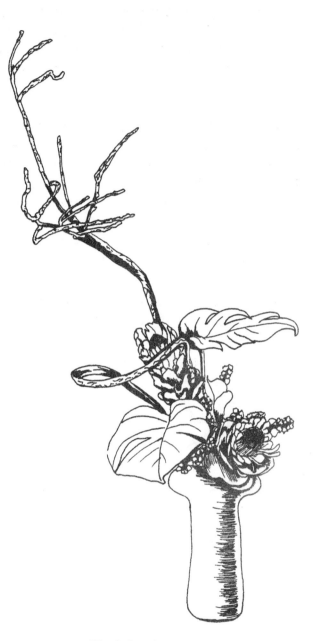

Korinka Arrangements
Figure 13

Korinka Arrangement
Figure 14

Moribana Omission Arrangement

Figure 15

*Flowers are the moment's*
*representations of things that*
*are in themselves eternal.*

*Sri Aurobindo*

## *Chapter Six*

## Nature's Message Through Symbolism And Color

History is replete with the symbolism attributed to nature. Cultures, races, and spiritual groups have long attached significance to flowers, trees, and shrubs. Why? Grohmann writes that the flower does not possess an individual soul as does the human, yet its impact is upon the soul. "The soul forces in the plant kingdom do not bestow inner feeling, but out form. These soul forces become a projected picture which through colour and form appeal to our senses. Most striking is the flower, which of all the parts of the plant is closest to our soul. This is why some flowers strike us as symbols of soul qualities."[1]

Transformative artist, Ilana Lilienthal believes that each flower emits a specific 'aura' or energy field which impacts the human consciousness. In describing her paintings of flower auras she says, "Each flower expresses itself to me in its own way, and my main focus is to translate the specific soul energy unique to each flower. It is this specific soul energy that touches and affects people. Different paintings, like different flowers, speak to people depending on their need."[2]

Flowers speak to our heart, the organ associated with feeling, and for this reason are given as gifts to express various sentiments. Thomas Hood expresses this in his poem, "The Language of Flowers":

> Yet, no not words, for they
> But half can tell love's feeling;
> Sweet flowers alone can say
> What passion fears revealing.
> A once bright rose's wither'd leaf,
> A tow'ring lily broken-
> Oh, these may paint a grief
> No words could e'er have spoken.[3]

Symbology traveled from the Orient to Europe, where first the French and then the English popularized an entire language of flowers. Importance was attached to the way in which a flower was presented—upright, to indicate the meaning of the flowers; inverted if the opposite thought was to be conveyed.[4] A flower worn in a woman's hair, cleavage, or over her heart had the significance of caution, friendship, or love respectively.[5] Many variations of secret messages were developed and practiced, especially during the reign of Queen Victoria in the 1840's.

More important than a code of presentation, however, is the meaning given to each flower. The Orient is credited for most symbology attributed to nature; indeed its peoples seem to have an inherent closeness that has enabled them to understand the heart of nature.

The chrysanthemum, known as the "Flower of Four Seasons," is revered in both Japan and China. An annual festival is held each year in Japan to celebrate this flower. The Japanese believe that its form symbolizes the sun, while China attributes to it the meaning of longevity. In India, life energy is held to be its significance.[6]

The lotus is considered a sacred flower in India, and its meanings are manifold. It has been described by some to indicate life and death; the past, present, and future; divine consciousness, purity, and truth. It is also a symbol of the human being who begins his life in the mud of materialism; who must rise through the waters of illusion; and blossom in the spiritual light.[7]

The lily (white) in all cultures speaks of purity. It is also considered "...the sense picture of the new birth of man in Christ."[8] There are a variety of lilies, however, which bring to mind different interpretations. The lemon day-lily, for example, means to forget your troubles, while the legend of the tiger lily tells the story of a hermit who befriended a tiger, upon whose death the Gods turned into a lily which grew by the hermit's cave.[9]

The blue forget-me-not implies its meaning of true love. A legend is told of two lovers walking alongside a river bank when the beautiful blue flowers were sighted floating on the water. The young man jumped into the river to retrieve the blossoms for his maiden. As the river carried him down stream, he tossed the flowers to the bank saying, "forget me not."[10]

The rose is believed to have been created by the Greek goddess of flowers, Chloris, assisted by Aphrodite, the goddess of love; Dionysus, the god of wine, and the three Graces—each contributing to its beauty, fragrance, and charm.[11] The rose is deemed a special flower in the cultures of both East and West. Its meaning in the Orient is love for the divine; in the West, love and beauty. The rose is most often used for occasions of celebrations where the sentiment of love is especially important such as weddings, anniversaries, and Valentine's Day. A custom of giving roses on this day has been popularized in the West. The tulip, another popular flower associated with Valentine's Day, is said to be a declaration of love.[12]

Ivy speaks to the heart of friendship and marriage, and is often used in a bride's bouquet. Rosemary is for remembrance. It's stimulating fragrance 'wakes you up.' The whimsical form of the columbine suggests folly, while the fragrant and lovely narcissus represents self-love and conceit. The iris is felt to dispel evil spirits and to prevent the spread of disease. This flower expresses both delicate beauty and strength of will—out of its strength the beauty emerges. The bearded iris is known in France as a fleur-de-lys, which is named after Louis the Seventh who wore the iris as his coat of arms. It is considered to be the aristocracy of beauty.[13]

"He loves me-he loves me not," is a phrase often used in plucking the petals of a daisy, and is a symbol of innocence and shared sentiments. The daisy has always reminded me of freedom, spontaneity, and joyful activity. It is also reputed to be the flower of the "Maid Marguerite, meek and mild" of Antioch. It was said that she saved many lives of those soon to be mothers through her prayers.[14]

One of my favorite flowers to arrange is the protea. The protea is indigenous to South Africa where it grows as prevalent as weeds. Due to its variety of species and form, it received its name from the Greek God Proteus who had the ability to prophecise the future, and to change his form at will to elude those who sought to know their fate.[15] I believe that the protea carries an extra message of transformation, and I like to use it in an arrangement for someone who is ill. A change is required in order for an individual to be healed, and the protea is a symbol of the transformation that is possible.

I have found the most beautiful flower stories to come from Corinne Heline in her book, *Magic Gardens*. She tells how the lily of the valley came to be known as the crown-of-motherhood; of the sacrifice and service of the mistletoe; how the jasmine reflects divine peace, and the white rose, a herald for all those souls who wish to be born in the coming year. So much can be conveyed to the human soul through a single flower. Sri Aurobindo said, "Flowers are the moment's representations of things that are in themselves eternal."[16] When we make a flower arrangement, we are arranging eternal truths. We are arranging what lives in our soul as feeling and in the flower as form. This relationship awakens and heals.

Flowers speak to our heart in a universal language. I had this experience while attending a study session in flower arranging in Japan. My instructors spoke only Japanese, I only English, and my interpreter, primarily Japanese. So we communicated through the flowers in my arrangement, and each understood what the other was saying. This would not have been possible if the flowers themselves did not contain universal truths.

By their form, certain flowers and plants also portray a symbolic relationship to the insect and animal kingdom, which has led to their name. There is, for example, the bee orchid, the spider mum, the snapdragon, the bird of paradise, the tiger lily, cattails, horsetail, and snake plant. At times, flowers or plants are given a name that has reminded the originator of a stereotyped characteristic. One that comes to mind is a rather strong and inflexible pointed leaf, affectionately referred to as mother-in-law's tongue.

Trees also stand before us as living symbols of truth. Each is said to have its own spirit which remains with it unto its death.[17] According to van Gelder, who could see and communicate with these tree spirits, they assist in sustaining the life of the tree by directing its energies, and influencing the chemical processes by its sense of well-being.[18] What I found most interesting is that the spirit can separate itself and step away from its tree, which it does most frequently in the evening, and at other intervals when given cause.[19] Most tree spirits have affectionate feelings for human beings and can even go searching a few feet for a human friend. This realization gives even greater meaning and joy in being out in nature.

Dorothy Maclean is another who has experienced the living consciousness of the trees, and has communicated with the tree Devas. A Deva is not the individual tree spirit, but has defined itself as "the overlighting intelligence of each species."[20] In one communication, Maclean was given this message from the Scots pine:

> ....Trees, rooted guardians of the surface, converters of the higher forces to Earth through the ground, have a special gift for man in this age of speed and drive and busy-ness. We are calmness, strength, endurance, praise, and fine attunement, all of which are greatly needed in the world. We are more than that. We are expressions of the love of the Creator for his abundant, unique and related life. We have purpose. We could not do without one another however isolated or self-

sufficient we may be geographically. The whole of life is here now, and it is our privilege to sound our special note. Come to our side whenever you can, and lift your consciousness.[21]

Trees contribute to the health of humankind through their forces, their beauty, and their symbolism. It is for this reason that persons who are exhausted and ill are advised to take up residence in nature's surroundings. The current deforestation occurring over the earth not only affects the ecological balance of life and disrupts life sustaining forces, it also removes the assistance trees give to humankind in helping us to maintain our health on a daily basis.

An example of the trees' assistance is seen in a study by Roger Ulrich of the University of Delaware. Ulrich researched the effect a hospital room view had on the recovery of gall bladder surgical patients. Twenty-three patients had a view of trees and foliage, while the other twenty-three looked at a brick wall. He found that those who viewed the trees required less medication, were more agreeable patients to the nursing staff, and had a shorter hospital stay.[23]

Trees desire to be acknowledged as living realities with a purpose in the divine drama just as each human being has its purpose. The trees will only communicate, however, with those who will raise their consciousness in reverence to them.

> The talking oak
> To the ancient spoke,
>
> But any tree
> Will talk to me
>
> What truth I know
> I garnered so.

But those who want to talk and tell,
And those who will not listeners be,
Will never hear a syllable
From out the lips of any tree.[24]

Joyce Kilner wrote, "I think that I shall never see a poem as lovely as a tree..." [25]   By appreciating their presence and beauty, we open ourselves to the message they bring.

The oak was significant in the ritual of the Druids of Britain, as is the cypress in Buddhist and Shinto ceremonies of the Orient. The cypress is considered to be the most ancient of trees, referred to as the tree of the gods. The pine, due to its evergreen nature throughout the seasons, represents longevity, endurance, and health. In Japan, an arrangement using pine is always made to celebrate the New Year and to bring good luck. Bamboo speaks of filial piety, friendship, fidelity, and longevity. The bamboo bends with the storms and grows stronger as it grows older. The maple tree clearly portrays the seasons through the changing color of its leaves. The Japanese maple is especially beautiful in the fall, and is very calming when used in an arrangement.[26]

The weeping willow can be used in arrangements to express grief and mourning, while the curly or crooked willow is used to celebrate happy occasions such as a marriage or a journey. The willow is also associated with Kannon, the goddess of mercy and compassion, who is said to have used this branch to sprinkle the nectars of life upon the sick.[27] The willow is a favorite branch material of most students and instructors as it has so much movement and life.

The plum tree heralds the arrival of spring as it is

94

among the first to appear through the snow. It represents courage, purity, virtue, and faith. The camellia branch and flower are known as perfected loveliness. The branches are especially prized due to the shape of the leaves, its color of green, and its longevity in an arrangement.[28]

Even though we regard nature in feminine gender calling her Mother, the Orient recognizes both principles, male and female, working in harmony to create its balance. Gregory Conway in *Flowers: East-West*, tells us that trees are considered masculine and small flowers feminine. The perfect flower is thought to be masculine which parallels the truism that we see in animals of the male species being the more colorful or beautiful. Branches as well as leaves have a positive and negative or a masculine and feminine side to them, and are arranged accordingly. The positive side, as a rule, shows the branch and leaf's greatest beauty.

Some may view this philosophy as sexist in our contemporary times, but it is based upon the understanding and respect for both masculine and feminine principles at work in the universe. There is no competition here or derogatory meanings intended. The masculine and feminine principles have different energies and functions which will manifest in a way suitable for their expression. Their symbology or appearance can, therefore, be seen in nature and even in the structure and function of our human bodies. We would not see these parallels if the masculine and feminine principles were not based upon a higher cosmology than what we entertain in our everyday consciousness.

In making an arrangement, the duality of principles are brought together to form a unity which serves as an example for us humans to balance the masculine and feminine sides of our self, and to carry that balance into our human relationships.

Nature speaks to us of principles, qualities and virtues, and serves as an example in conducting our human life. Okada said, "Nature is a great teacher...When we observe it closely, study its ways, we should be able to perceive the true meaning of almost all human affairs."[29] One example given by Okada references human impasses and the bamboo. Okada compares impasses to the joints of a bamboo stalk.[30] The bamboo receives its strength from the joints on its stalk, which occur at intervals during its cycle of growth. Without these impasses, which he considers turning points, the human being, like the bamboo without joints, would be weak. It is due to its joints that the bamboo can weather the storms of nature; likewise, the times of challenge, the quieter periods of reflection or turning points, enable humans to weather the storms of life.

From a human perspective most perceive the periods of expansion in their life to be the most productive because there appears to be greater activity and growth. However, relating Okada's teaching through nature, the quiet activities and those with obstacles (contraction) are what give us strength and prepare us to go forward into times of expansion. The cycle of expansion and contraction provides a rhythm like breathing itself, and is not unlike the growth of the plant. This rhythm enables the individual to move forward in life with greater balance and wisdom.

Itsuki Okada relates an analogy of fallen leaves of the camphor trees to human mistakes. "Just as camphor trees grow more because the leaves they have dropped act as fertilizers, so our mistakes and failures help us to grow. Not realizing this, we often indulge in regret and worry over our failures, so much we stop growing and become stagnant...When we realize our mistakes or failures, we should drop them like dead leaves and go ahead to our next task happily and positively."[31]

A rose doesn't bloom all the time. It, too, has its cycle of contraction and expansion, of life and death. Like a flower we are born into the world and must also depart from it. The sun always rises in the East and sets in the West. Humankind, being of spirit, soul, and body finds itself reborn into the world of spirit once the physical body is discarded. Death is not a void or an end, but a beginning that unfolds on another level of being.

"To every thing there is a season, and a time to every purpose under the heaven."[32] The timing and order that prevails in nature causes us to reflect on our own life. Do we wait for the right time to begin a new task, or do we force things prematurely. Anyone who has failed understands the importance of right timing. Nature is punctual in its growth, unlike the tendency for human beings to frequently be late. What would happen to the growth of the plant if its forces were always late? If the undines were not there to take up their task from the gnomes, or the sylphs from the undines, or the salamanders from the sylphs? Okada indicated that God's plan goes on with or without us. It is our responsibility to heed nature and to be on time.

We can always learn something from nature through quiet observation. When humankind abides by the laws of nature inherent in its growth, harmony prevails. The tree or flower begins as a seed and progresses through stages of growth in order to fulfill its purpose.

We can apply this natural pattern to the undertaking of any project, and also to our own cycles of growth and individual purpose. While it has become increasingly difficult for persons to find their life task, Great Nature serves as an example of purpose in all its variations.

> The Pine lives for a thousand years,
> The Morning Glory but for a single day:
> Yet both have fulfilled their destiny.[23]

Nature speaks in silent symbolism. It also speaks through color. Steiner said, "Colour is the soul of Nature and the Cosmos, and we become aware of this soul when we experience colour."[34] We see color through our eyes but we experience it in our soul, which provides a healing impulse to the spirit. Shades of green everywhere in nature reflect a quiet and calm harmony which has a similar effect on our soul, one which refreshes and balances. The array of colored flowers also speaks to us in a myriad of ways. Every flower has a colored aura which symbolizes different qualities and can alter its meaning and soul response.

The question must then be asked, "What is the nature of color that it causes a response in our soul?" The answer cannot be obtained from Isaac Newton whose theory in 1666 suggests that color is created through refraction of sunlight. His definition of color as split-up light and so many wave-lengths vibrating per second does not address the true life of color. Johann Wolfgang von Goethe, however, provides a qualitative study of color which includes moral and physiological implications important to understanding its impact upon the soul. Of all Goethe's accomplishments, he valued his *Theory of Colours* (1810) as his finest achievement. This work was later expanded upon by Rudolf Steiner.

Goethe depicted the nature of color as that which arises from the interplay of light and dark. Darkness, to Goethe, is a force which serves as the polarity of light. An example of this weaving of forces is demonstrated at sunrise and sunset.

Goethe identified yellow and blue as the two basic or primordial colors—yellow being closer to the light, and blue, closer to the darkness.[35] Color is in movement according to Goethe, and a spectrum of color arises from each, the yellow and the blue, as a result of an intensification of the preceding color. Yellow moves through to red-yellow and yellow-red, while blue intensifies to red-blue and blue-red.[36] Yellow and blue then meet in green.[37]

Goethe also indicated that colors are impressed upon the mind, and particular feelings are evoked in response to a specific color. Those on the light side excite feelings which are "quick, lively, aspiring," while those on the darker side, "bring on a restless, susceptible, anxious impression."[38] Yellow in its pure state has the quality of "brightness, and has a serene, gay, softly exciting character; red-yellow impresses warmth and gladness; yellow-red produces an extreme excitement."[39] Blue in its pure state is a quality of "stimulating negation...a contradiction between excitement and repose...it seems to retire from us but draws us after it...it gives us the impression of cold or shade."[40] Red-blue "does not enliven so much as it unsettles," while blue-red (magenta or reddish purple) may make a serious and dignified impression or one of grace and charm."[41]

Goethe's work was further substantiated in 1920 by a German psychiatrist, Willem Zeylmans Van mmichoven, who researched the psychological influence of color on his patients and concluded the following:

> Whereas we see with yellow and golden yellow feelings of happiness and cheefulness next to a light stimulating effect, we see with blue feelings that have a clear calming effect next to a feeling of seriousness and sadness. The lightness of the color has been felt with the yellows, the darkness with the blues. The polarities of feelings become bigger when on both sides red is included. With the orange red and red the light stimulus grows to excitement that is sometimes sexual and passionate, sometimes merely pleasing. The feelings of happiness and cheerfulness become stronger the color is felt as warm and comes towards the person. With the blue violet and violet the effect is more clear and the feelings of sadness deepen. In magenta (reddish purpose) we see both opposites connected. Next to the highest degree of excitement we see very deep, serious feelings. In green the opposites almost disappear. So we have a light calming effect next to a sense of happiness.[42]

We breathe in the colors we see and respond with a feeling. Not all ages experience the same phenomenon however. Steiner indicated, that unlike adults, young children inwardly experience the complementary or opposite color of what they see outwardly. This has led to the practice of dressing some excitable children in red so that they experience the calming effect of the color green.[43] Goethe explained the phenomenon of complementary colors as arising out of the eye's need for completeness, "...the eye relieves itself by producing the opposite of the single colour forced upon it, and thus attains the entire impression which is so satisfactory to it."[44]

An exercise Steiner gave to demonstrate the complementary colors, which I use in my classes, is to paint a circle of yellow, red, and blue on separate piece of white paper. One of the colors is held up for viewing for several seconds, after which it is replaced by a blank, white paper. The after image, or complementary color, appears against the background of white paper. My students are often amazed at what they experience.

We often use complementary colors in our arrangements, the yellow-purple combination being especially popular. As a rule, the use of flowers is limited to two or three varieties or colors in an arrangement. Given the choice of using more green or more flowers, the general rule is to use more green because that is what prevails in nature. The use of too many colors is disturbing to the harmony of the arrangement. It becomes too busy, sending out many messages at one time so perhaps none are received.

Students frequently ask how to select the right combination of colors for their flower arrangements. The process of color selection can be intellectualized by using a color-wheel and working with hues (the name of the color family such as blue), values (degrees of light or darkness), and intensity (strong or weak), but I prefer the approach of "feeling" what colors are appropriate together and in harmony with the vase. Colors have a movement, gesture, or quality peculiar to each which, in turn, evokes particular feelings within the soul of the observer. An example of the colors' gesture is communicated in this color verse by educator, Alstan Hegg:

> Blue with love is all embracing
> Yellow selflessly is shining
> Green between them shows the living
> Red with warmth and life is moving
> Orange courage strong is showing
> Purple gives its royal blessing

Indigo the depths are shading
Black shows lifelessness and dying
While in peach the soul is glowing
And in brown they are all mixing
Colors living: Colors breathing.
Colors moving: Colors fading
Stimulate imagination
And inspire our creating.[45]

When selecting flower color combinations, the question can be asked if the color of a flower is warm or cool. Color is a living process, and each one's gesture indicates its activity or rest. Does the color's movement radiate outward like the glowing sun, or does it recede and draw you after it like the blue sky? By allowing the gesture of the color to rise up within, a student can determine if a color combination is appropriate or not. Once again, nature is the teacher, and learning comes through observation and experience.

Different occasions often suggest the colors of flowers to be used. For example, white flowers are used most frequently for weddings, funerals, and to celebrate the seasons of Christmas and Easter. The symbolic meaning of a white flower is purity. The color white, according to Steiner, is the image of the spirit. White flowers in an arrangement appear very pure and still. There is a centering and a sacred feeling that accompanies their presence. Black, on the other hand, in Steiner's color science, is the image of the lifeless. We frequently use black vases which seem to highlight the flowers, but rarely use this color in our arrangements. There are exceptions, however. The black calla lily which springs up as a volunteer and is rarely seen, can be arranged in an appropriate vase and appreciated for its unusual and striking beauty. At Halloween, I enjoy combining one or two dried lily-of-the-nile flowers with their black seeds exposed, with orange flowers to set the mood for this occasion. We learn from folklore that this celebration had its origin in the Celtic festival of Samhain, November 1st, on the eve of which it was believed that the spirits of the dead, witches, and others roamed about.[46] Using something of black is appropriate at this time.

Conway relates the Japanese interpretation of colors to the masculine and feminine principle. The colors of white, yellow, and blue are believed to aspire toward the feminine, while the red, pink, purple and variegated tones—stronger colors—represent its masculine counterpart.

When we design arrangements for exhibitions which are displaying other art forms such as paintings and sculpture, we coordinate the flowers and vases with these works of art and the surroundings. In addition to the arrangement's own beauty and value as a work of art, this coordination enhances the artistic quality of the other pieces, and enlivens the space of the gallery. It is more important for us to create a work of art that is in harmony with itself and the environment, than be too concerned for what a color may indicate.

We glean from Goethe and Steiner's writings in what way the soul responds to the colors we experience in nature and in our flower arrangements. Observers will feel a sense of life and tranquility in the midst of nature's colors. Blair Justice writes:

> Various studies have shown that nature scenes—views of water and vegetation, particularly—elicit positive feelings in people, reduce anxiety in those who are stressed and significantly increase the amplitude of alpha brain waves. High alpha amplitude is associated with feelings of relaxation. When we experience beauty, then, we seem less likely to have stressful thoughts and physiological arousal.[47]

Colored flowers will often be favorites of some and not of others. Just as the flowers have a colored aura, the human astral body is one of changing color, from which a color aura is projected. In *Colour and Healing*, Gladys Mayer writes, "...the soul strives towards the colours it longs to acquire, but has not yet achieved in its own aura."[48] At other times, the color is one that has already found expression in one's life. At Sangetsu exhibits individuals will usually comment about their favorite arrangement on display, which speaks to me of something that lives within them.

In Sangetsu we utilize the dynamics of color to create arrangements that are therapeutic, providing healing through color as well as form. After a few classes, my students often comment that their perception of nature has changed. They see colors, lines, and rhythms of which they were not previously aware. A former student writes:

> I view nature differently now than from before Sangetsu. I am more appreciative. I notice positive-negative sides; I see the [asymmetrical] triangle even in garden arrangements, and have come to appreciate plants and branches that I had ordinarily overlooked. I perceive and acknowledge a reverence for life.[49]

As a result of arranging flowers, a change in consciousness has occurred bringing about a transformation in that individual's life. Mayer speaks of the role color plays in this process of awakening individuals to increased sensitivity: "Through an awakened sense of color, one begins to awaken to the world around us in a new way...Colour speaks to us, and our soul's response is a renewed joy in living."[50] Our soul breathes in the living color and symbolism of the flowers we arrange, and in the process we become more alive.

*"Just living is not enough,"*
*said the butterfly. "One*
*must have sunshine, freedom,*
*and a little flower."*

Hans Christian Andersen


*Chapter Seven*


# Conclusion


I am an instructor of Sangetsu but I am also a student. It is my belief that no one ever arrives at a point of completion in regards to nature or the art of flower arranging. Nature constantly improves and renews itself, and we must follow a similar process. Students come to Sangetsu through various avenues. They have read of a class being offered, seen an exhibit and want to learn, or have a friend taking the class who has recommended it. I saw a Sangetsu arrangement for the first time at a center for Johrei Fellowship* in Los Angeles in 1975. I was inspired by its quiet beauty, arranged so simply to express each branch and flower's unique quality, and I wanted to learn how to create a work of art such as the one I was standing before.

*Johrei Fellowship was founded by Okada to construct a better world through the practice of Johrei (a spiritual healing), nature farming (growing food without chemicals and pesticides), and the appreciation of art and beauty.

It was not long after that I journeyed to Japan. While walking near the plum garden at the international headquarters which houses Sangetsu, I came to rest upon a step, and there by my feet lay a beautiful pink camellia. Its appearance seemed rather mysterious as I had not noticed any others around. Attaching some importance to my find, I carried the flower with me to my other destinations that morning. Each time I set it down one petal remained behind in my hand. I placed the blossom in what I determined to be a safe place while attending a meeting, but upon my return it was nowhere to be found. What remained of the experience were three petals which I held in my hand.

The camellia has since had special meaning for me, and led me to believe that I had a purpose to fulfill in regards to flowers. I began my study of Sangetsu flower arranging in the Spring of 1976. It was not until 1982 that I became an instructor and began teaching in Long Beach, California.

In 1983, more than in other years, I became conscious of changes that had occurred in me—changes in temperament, feelings, responses, awareness, and abilities. One of the biggest revelations came during a Sangetsu study session and visit to the MOA Museum of Art that year in Atami, Japan. I viewed artifacts I had seen numerous times at the museum in Hakone (which had since been transferred to Atami). In previous tours, I had whizzed by these "National Treasures" and "Important Cultural Properties" with no particular feeling. This visit, however, was different. I was mesmerized by the art and remained with just two pieces, the statue of Prince Shotoku at age two, and the Wisteria Vase by Ninsei for well over an hour. My consciousness of beauty had expanded dramatically.

I was also working at the time as a manager of an arts program in Long Beach. In spite of having a limited art background other than flower arranging, I realized that I had developed an eye for selecting art, and could feel the flow and space necessary for its best display. I also experienced a greater awareness of nature, its myriad colors, textures, and forms. Through the years of arranging flowers my personality has become more balanced. I no longer fluctuate between extremes, but have come to rest somewhere in the middle.

As an instructor, I have also observed changes among my Sangetsu students, immediate and those of longer term. Frequently, students come to class tired, stressed, or otherwise upset about something that has occurred during the day. By the end of the class, however, there has been a transformation. They are smiling, appear more relaxed, have more vitality and color in their face, and are happy they made the effort to attend. In the space of just one class the flowers have performed a valuable service of healing.

I have also observed that the degree of healing that takes place in class often depends on how an instructor facilitates the process. That love for our flowers is more important than technique is an important guide. I have noticed that if too much technique is given, or the critiquing of arrangements is too strict, the student's experience is not as positive, and can be, at times, frustrating. The instructor must create a harmonious space for the students to be centered in the beauty and the energy of the flowers, and to express their creativity within the confines of the materials.

Arranging flowers affects people's lives and environment. The understanding that nature and beauty assist in the healing process led the Menninger Clinic in Topeka, Kansas, founded by Drs. C.F., Karl, and William Menninger in 1925 for the treatment of mental-emotional disorders, to institute horticulture as one of their therapeutic activities with significant success. The program has demonstrated that being in nature and working with the trees, flowers, and plants, impacts all levels of a person's being, and provides a positive catalyst for change. Horticulture programs now exist at various hospitals, care centers, and prisons throughout the country.

Okada said, "Truly beautiful environments are a great help toward inspiring more beautiful thoughts in the minds of the public, which will greatly reduce crime and other evils in society."[1] The arrangement of a single flower can effect a transformation, and Okada had a vision of flowers playing a significant role in transforming people's lives on a large scale:

> We wish to encourage people to cultivate flowers and to distribute them as the best method for the popularization of beauty. This begins with decorating the rooms in our individual homes and in other buildings. It is true that we see flowers placed in many middle- and upper-class homes, but we feel this is not enough. Our aim is to encourage everyone to place arrangements in every place of every kind, so wherever people go they will see flowers and enjoy them.[2]

The Sangetsu School of Flower Arranging is working toward the fulfillment of this aim. The simplicity of Okada's guidelines— to arrange flowers naturally according to their growth patterns and inherent beauty; to arrange flowers quickly so that they do not loose their life forces and vitality; to arrange flowers as if painting a picture, with the placement of each one a different stroke

108

of the brush onto the canvas; to arrange flowers
harmony with the vase and its placement; and to arran
flowers with joy—makes it possible for anyone to mak
beautiful and healing arrangements.

As an individual's spiritual being is purified, and
his/her knowledge of how to arrange flowers naturally
and skillfully increases, her arrangements will emit a
greater light-energy in ever expanding circles of influence.

Many of our students, in addition to making arrangements for their home, take one to their place of
work or other public facility. They do so in a spirit of joy
in which the flowers were arranged. This spirit of joy is
also expressed by the nature spirits and devas as they
assist in the growth process of nature. Joy permeates the
life of nature, and nature, in turn, gives its joy and
healing to humankind. This is the way of Great Nature.
This is the way of Sangetsu.

*A large camellia*
*Was blooming in my garden.*
*I cut, arranged it,*
*And put it in the alcove*
*What joy I felt in living.*[3]

## Chapter One Notes:

1    Okada, M., "Meishu-sama's Thoughts About the Art of Flower Arranging," in <u>Sangetsu School of Flower Arranging Instructor's Manual for Spiritual Guidance</u>, p.16.

2    Okada, M., "Plants Are Alive," <u>Sangetsu</u>, op.cit.:12.

3    Okada, M., "Plants Have Consciousness," <u>Foundations of Paradise</u>, pp.273-74.

4    Ibid.:274.

5    Okada, Itsuki, "Basic Rules of Flower Arranging," <u>Sangetsu</u>, op.cit.:44.

6    Okada, M., "Plants Are Alive," Sangetsu, op.cit.:13

7    Okada, "Why My Flowers Last," <u>Sangetsu</u>, op.cit.:22- 23.

8    Ibid.:23.

9    Okada, "All in Harmony," <u>Sangetsu</u>, op.cit.:17.

10    Okada, <u>True Health</u>, p.172.

11    Okada, "All in Harmony," <u>Sangetsu</u>, op.cit.:17.

12    Okada, M., <u>Prayers and Gosanka</u>, p.75.

## Chapter Two Notes:

1    Carr, Rachel, E., <u>Japanese Floral Art</u>, p.32.

2    Okada, M. "The Power of Nature," in <u>Foundation of Paradise</u>, p.50

3    Okada, "The Elements of Fire, Water and Soil," <u>Foun dation</u>, op.cit.:53.

4    Ibid.

5    Ibid.

6    Okada, M., <u>True Health</u>, p. 110.

7    Ibid.:111.

8    Ibid.

9    Okada, M.,"The Elements of Fire, Water and Soil," in <u>Foundation</u>, op.cit.53

10    Okada, M., <u>True</u>, op.cit.:110.

11    Okada, M., "Climate and Weather," <u>Teachings of Meishu-Sama</u>, Vol I, p.59.

12    Okada, M. "The Power of Nature," in <u>Foundation</u>, op.cit.:52.

13    Buhler, Walter, <u>Living With Your Body</u>, p.12.

14    Okada, "Johrei and the Three-Element Composition of

the Internal Organs," in <u>True Health</u>, p.110, and "The
Elements of Fire, Water, and Soil, " in <u>Foundation</u>,
op.cit.:54.

15      Ibid.
16      Ibid.
17      Ibid.
18      Okada, "The Elements of Fire, Water and Soil," in
        <u>Foundation</u>, op.cit.:55.
19      Okada, Itsuki, <u>Sangetsu School of Flower Arranging
        Instructor's Manualfor Spiritual Guidance</u>, p.31.
20      <u>Sangetsu School of Flower Arranging</u>, Vol 5, p.36.
21      Howard, Susan, Loa Tsu quote cited in <u>Advanced Souls</u>.
22      Okada, M., <u>Teachings of Meishu-Sama</u>, Vol. I., p.12.

## Chapter Three Notes:

1       Leonardo da Vinci, edited by Jean Paul Richter, <u>The
        Notebooks of Leonardo Da Vinci</u>, Vol II, pp.220-221. I
        have chosen a more literary translation and have tried
        unsuccessfully to determine its source.  A
        translation of this quotation can be found in the source
        just listed.
2        ZaJonc, Arthur G., "The Wearer of Shapes- Goethe's
        Study of Clouds and Weather," <u>Orion Nature Quarterly</u>,
        Winter, 1984. p.40.
3       Steiner, Rudolf, <u>Health and Illness</u>, Vol. II, p.123.
4       Ibid.:122.
5       Steiner, Rudolf, <u>Fundamentals of Anthroposophical
        Medicine</u>, p.44.
6       Ibid.
7       Ibid.:46
8       Gorter, Robert, lecture, "Threefold/fourfold Man,"
        August 29, 1987.
9       Ibid.
10      Ibid.
11      Gorter, Robert, lecture, "Anthroposophical Medicine,"
        March 23, 1981.
12      Ibid.
13      Ibid.
14      Bentheim, et al., op.cit.:29.
15      Grohmann, Gerbert, <u>The Plant</u>, p.120.
16      Ibid.:92.

17    Grohmann, op.cit.:111.
18    Steiner, Rudolf, Foundations of Esotericism, p.16.
19    Ibid.:18.
20    Grohmann, op.cit.:113.
21    Ibid.:115
22    Husemann, F., and Wolff, O., The Anthroposophical Approach To Medicine.Volume I, p. 318.
23    Grohmann, op.cit.:54.
24    Bentheim, et all., op.cit.:36.
25    Nesfield-Cookson, Bernard, citing Rudolf Steiner in, Rudolf Steiner'sVision of Love, p. 175.
26    Bailey, Alice, "Joy" in Ponder On This, p.228.
27    MacLean, Dorothy, To Hear The Angels Sing, p.54.

## Chapter Four Notes:

1    Steiner, Rudolf, The Wisdom of Man of the Soul, and of the Spirit, p.93.
2    Okada, M., "Man's Three Spirits," in Teachings of Meishu-Sama, Vol. II, p. 37.
3    Ibid.:37-38.
4    Ibid.:37.
5    Okada, M., Sounds of the Dawn, Vol II, p.178.
6    Okada, M., "Strata in the Spiritual Realm," in Teach ings of Meishu-Sama, Vol. I, p.26.
7    Okada, M., "The Spiritual Cord," in Teachings of Meishu-Sama, Vol I, p.47.
8    Okada, M., "The Spiritual Cord," in Foundation of Paradise, p.56.
9    Steiner, R., Theosophy, p.68.
10    Ibid.:37.
11    Steiner, R. Occult Science, pp.21-34.
12    Ibid.:26.
13    Steiner, R. The Four Temperaments, p.24.
14    Ibid.:25.
15    Steiner, R. Occult Science, pp.41-42.
16    Okada, Foundation op. cit.:275.
17    Okada, Sounds op. cit.:247.
18    Frankl, Elizabeth, citing Lilienthal, Ilana, "Painting The Souls of Flowers," in East West Magazine, May 1989, p.44.

9   Klein, Adrian Bernard, <u>Colour-Music The Art of Light</u>, p. p.32.
20  Steiner, R., <u>Art In The Light Of Mystery Wisdom</u>, p.22.
21  Maclean, Dorothy, <u>To Hear the Angels Sing</u>, p. 94.
22  Lush, Jean with Patricia Rushford, "Women of Beauty and the Essence of Mystique," p.3, in <u>Focus on the Family</u>, May 1987 (article exerpted from her book, <u>Emotional Phases of a Woman's Life</u>).
23  Ibid.
24  Justice, Blair, <u>Who Gets Sick</u>, p.262.
25  Okada, Itsuki, "Art in Daily Life," citing M. Okada in <u>Sangetsu School of Flower Arranging, Instructor's Manual For Spiritual Guidance</u>, p.38.
26  Steiner,R., <u>Art</u> op.cit.:101.
27  Ibid.:103
28  Ibid.:108-109.
29  Steiner, Occult Science, p.40.
30  Unpublished correspondence, Wakayama Women's Prison Inmates,1983-1988; names withheld in the interest of privacy.
31  Sakamoto, Hiroko, unpublished correspondence, 1989.
32  Unpublished correspondence, Long Beach Sangetsu Students, 1982-1988; names withheld in the interest of privacy.
33  Okada, <u>Teachings</u>, Vol 11, op.cit.:27.
34  Ibid.:28
35  Husemann, Friedrich, M.D., <u>Goethe and the Art of Healing</u>, p.163.

## Chapter Five Notes:

1   Husemann, Friedrich, M.D., <u>Goethe and the Art of Healing</u>, p.57.
2   Ibid.:53.
3   Ibid.
4   Goethe, Johann Wolfgang von, <u>The Metamorphosis of Plants</u>, p.9.
5   Husemann, op.cit.:57-58.
6   Goethe, op.cit.:20.
7   Goethe, op.cit.:18
8   Goethe, op.cit.:54.

9    Steiner, Rudolf, <u>Man as Symphony of the Creative Word</u>, p.120-134.
10   Ibid.:120.
11   Gelder, Dora van, <u>The Real World of Fairies</u>, p.43.
12   Steiner, op.cit.:124.
13   Ibid.:131.
14   Ibid.:128.
15   Roel, Janneheth, lecture on "Elementals," July, 18, 1987.
16   Gelder, op.cit.:back cover.
17   Ibid.:60.
18   Wachsmuth, Guenther, <u>Reincarnation</u>, p.159.
19   Ibid.:163.
20   Odent, Michel, M.D., "The Evolution of Obstetrics at Pithiviers," <u>Birth and The Family Journal</u>, Vol 8, Spring 1981; p.9.
21   Wachsmuth, op.cit.:194.
22   Steiner, Rudolf, <u>Essentials of Education</u>, p.78.
23   Okada, M., <u>Prayers and Gosanka</u>, p.81.

## Chapter Six Notes:

1    Grohmann, Gerbert, <u>The Plant</u>, p.119.
2    Frankl, Elizabeth citing Lilienthal, Ilana, in <u>EastWestJournal</u>, May 1989, p.42.
3    Powell, Claire, <u>The Meaning of Flowers</u>, p.17.
4    Ibid.:14.
5    Ibid.:15.
6    For these brief summaries of flower symbolism, I have condensed often repetitive (and consistently unreferenced) data taken from Gregory Conway, <u>Flowers: East-West</u>; Rachael Carr, <u>Japanese Floral Art</u>; The Mother, <u>Flowers and Their Messages</u>, A.S. Kull, <u>Secrets of Flowers</u>
7    Ibid.
8    Hiebel, Frederick, <u>Goethe's Message of Beauty</u>, p.15.
9    McKenny, Margaret and Johnston, Edith, <u>A Book of Garden Flowers</u>, published without page numbers.
10   Ibid.
11   Pickles, Sheila, <u>The Language of Flowers</u>, p.88.
12   Summaries, op.cit.
13   Summaries, op.cit.
14   Kull, A.S., <u>Secrets of Flowers</u>, p.21.
15   Eliovson, Sima, <u>Proteas For Pleasure</u>, p.3.

The Mother, citing Sri Aurobindo in <u>Flowers and Their Messages</u>, p.210.

17    Gelder, Dora van, <u>The Real World of Fairies</u>, p.63.

18    Ibid.

19    Ibid.

20    Maclean, Dorothy, <u>To Hear the Angels Sing</u>, p.50.

21    Ibid.:133.

22    Justice, Blair, <u>Who Gets Sick</u>, p. 262.

23    Ibid.:263

24    Heline, Corinne, <u>Magic Gardens</u>, citing Mary Davies, p.9.

25    Cook, Roy citing Joyce Kilmer in an anthology, <u>One Hundred and One Famous Poems</u>, p.39.

26    For these brief summaries of tree symbolism, I have condensed often repetitive ( and consistently unreferenced) data taken from Conway, op.cit; Carr, op.cit.

27    Carr, Rachael, <u>Japanese Floral Art</u>, p.86.

28    Summaries, Trees op.cit.

29    Okada, M., <u>Foundation of Paradise</u>, p.363.

30    Ibid.

31    Fujieda, Okada, Itsuki, "The Vibration of the Daylight Age," in <u>The Glory</u>,Number 58, p.5.

32    Ecclesiastes 3:1, <u>The Bible</u>, King James Version.

33    Suzuki, Daisetz, <u>Zen and Japanese Culture</u>, p.381.

34    Grohmann, op.cit.:20.

35    Goethe, Johann Wolfgang von, <u>Theory of Colours</u>, pp.306 & 310.

36    Ibid.:306;309-310.

37    Ibid.:316.

38    Ibid.:306.

39    Ibid.:306-310.

40    Ibid.:311.

41    Roel, Jannebeth, "Goethe's Color Theory in the Twentieth Century," unpublished paper, p.8.

42    Ibid.:6-7, citing Willem Zeylmans van Emmichoven.

43    Mayer, Gladys, <u>Colour and Healing</u>, p.45.

44    Goethe, <u>Theory</u>, op.cit.:319.

45    Hegg, Alstan, "Color Verse," unpublished poem.

46    Barz, Brigitte, <u>Festivals With Children</u>, p.93.

47    Justice, Blair, <u>Who</u>, op.cit.:262.

48    Mayer, Gladys, <u>Colour</u>, op.cit.:46.

49    Unpublished correspondence, Long Beach Sangetsu
      Students,    1982-1988; names withheld in the
      interest of privacy.
50    Mayer, op.cit.:41.

## Chapter Seven Notes:

1    Okada, M., "Paradise Is a World of Beauty," <u>Foundation
     of Paradise,</u> p. 257.
2    Okada, M., "The Role of Flowers in Establishing Para
     dise on Earth," op.cit.:272.
3    Okada, M., <u>Sangetsu School of Flower Arranging
     Instructor's Manual For Spiritual Guidance,</u> p.1.

# Copyright Acknowledgments

Rudolf Steiner Press and the Anthroposophical Society of London:exerpts from *Art In The Light of Mystery Wisdom* by Rudolf Steiner, copyright 1970; *Goethe and The Art of Healing* by Friedrich Husemann, M.D; *Man as Symphony of the Creative Word* by Rudolf Steiner, Copyright 1970.

Elizabeth Frankel, "*Painting the Souls of Flowers*,"a few lines reprinted with permission from *Natural Health: The Guide to Well-Being*, Box 1200, 17 Station Street, Brookline Village, MA 02147. Subscriptions $24/year. All rights reserved.

Jeremy P. Tarcher: an exerpt from *Who Gets Sick* by Blair Justice, copyright 1987. All rights reserved.

Alstan L. Hegg, "color verse," unpublished poem.

I also wish to thank Sangetsu students in Long Beach for permission to share their experiences, and Mrs. Hiroko Sakamoto for sending testimonials from her students at the Wakayama Womens Prison.

# BIBLIOGRAPHY

Bailey, Alice A. and Khul, Djwhal, <u>Ponder on This</u>, New York, London: Lucis Publishing Company, paperback edition, 1974.

Barz, Brigitte, <u>Festivals With Children</u>, Great Britain: Floris Books, 1987.

Bentheim, Tineke van, Bos, Saskia, et all, <u>Caring for the Sick at Home</u>, Edinburgh, Hudson: Anthroposophic Press, 1980.

Buhler, Walther, <u>Living With Your Body</u>, London: Rudolf Steiner Press, 1979.

Carr, Rachael, <u>Japanese Floral Art</u>, New York: Van Nostrand, 1961.

Conway, Gregory J., with Hiatt, Elinor Wallace, <u>Flowers: East-West</u>, New York, London: Alfred A. Knoph, 1938.

Ellovson, Sima, <u>Proteas For Pleasure</u>, Cape Town: Howard Timmins, 1965.

Gelder, Dora van, <u>The Real World of Fairies</u>, Wheaton, London: The Theosophical Publishing House, 1977.

Goethe, Johann Wolfgang von, <u>The Metamorphosis of Plants</u>, United States: Leo Fl. manfred Associates, Inc., 1978.

——————————, tr Charles Lock Eastlake, <u>Theory of Colours</u>, Cambridge, London: The M.I.T. Press, paperback edition, 1970.

Grohmann, Gerbert, <u>The Plant</u>, London: Rudolf Steiner Press, 1974.

Heline, Corinne, <u>Magic Gardens</u>, La Canada: New Age Press, 1974.

Husemann, Friedrich, M.D., tr., R.K. MacKaye and A. Goudschaal, <u>Goethe and the Art of Healing,</u> London, New York: The Rudolf Steiner Publishing Co.

Justice, Blair, Ph.D., <u>Who Gets Sick</u>, Los Angeles, New York: Jeremy P. Tarcher, Inc., 1987.

Klein, Adrian Bernard, <u>Colour-Music The Art of Light</u>, London: Crosby Lockwood and Son, 1926.

Kull, A. Stoddard, <u>Secrets of Flowers</u>, Brattleboro: the Stephen Green Press,1972.

Maclean, Dorothy, <u>To Hear the Angels Sing</u>, New York: Lindis Farne Press, 1988.

Mayer, Gladys, <u>Colour and Healing</u>, Sussex: New Knowledge Books, 1960.

——————, <u>Colour and The Human Soul</u>, Sussex: New Knowl edge Books, 1961.

McKenny, Margaret and Johnston, Edith F., <u>A Book of Garden Flowers</u>, New York: The Macmillan Company, 1940.

Mother, The, <u>Flowers and Their Messages</u>, Auroville: Sri Aurobindo Ashram Publication Department, 1979.

Nesfield-Cookson, Bernard, <u>Rudolf Steiner's Vision of Love</u>, Northamptonshire: The Aquarian Press, 1983.

Okada, Mokichi, <u>True Health</u>, United States: Church of World Messianity,1987.

——————, <u>Foundation of Paradise</u>: United States: Church of World  Messianity, 1984.

——————, <u>Teachings of Meishu-Sama</u>, Vol I, Los Angeles: Church of World Messianity, 1979.

——————, <u>Teachings of Meishu-Sama</u>, Vol II, Atami: Church of World Messianity, 1968.

—————————, tr. Lisa Taylor Melton, <u>Sounds of the Dawn</u>, Vol I, Atami: Church of World Messianity, 1971.

—————————, tr. Lisa Taylor Melton, <u>Sounds of the Dawn</u>, Vol II, Atami: Church of World Messianity, 1973.

—————————, <u>Prayers and Gosanka</u>, Los Angeles: Church of World Messianity, (year of publication not indicated).

Pickles, Sheila, <u>The Language of Flowers</u>, New York: Harmony Books, 1990.

Powell, Claire, <u>The Meaning of Flowers</u>, Boulder: Shambhala Publications, Inc., 1979.

Steiner, Rudolf, <u>Colour</u>, London: Rudolf Steiner Press, 1982.

—————————, <u>Man as Symphony of the Creative Word</u>, London: Rudolf Steiner Press, 1970.

—————————, <u>Foundations of Esotericism</u>, London: Rudolf Steiner Press, 1982.

—————————, <u>Fundamentals of Anthroposophical Medicine</u>, Spring Valley: Mercury Press, 1986.

—————————, <u>The Wisdom of Man of the Soul and of the Spirit</u>, New York: Anthroposophic Press, Inc., 1971.

—————————, tr., Johanna Collis, <u>Art In The Light Of Mystery Wisdom</u>, London: Rudolf Steiner Press, 1970.

—————————, <u>Occult Science</u>, Spring Valley: Anthroposophic Press, Inc., 1972.

—————————, <u>Theosophy</u>, New York: Anthroposophic Press, Inc., 1971.

—————————, <u>Health and Illness</u>, Vol II, Spring Valley: Anthroposophic Press, Inc., 1983.

——————, The Four Temperaments, New York:
Anthroposophic Press, Inc.,    1968.

——————, The Essentials of Education, London:
Anthroposophical Publishing   Company, 1926.

Suzuki, Daisetz, Zen and Japanese Culture, New York:  Pan
theon Books, 1959.

Wachsmuth, Guenther, Ph.D. tr., Olin D. Wannamaker, Rein
carnation, Dornach:    Philosophic-Anthroposophic
Press, 1937.

Compilations

Sangetsu School of Flower Arranging Instructor's Manual For
Spiritual Guidance. Church of World Messianity.

Sangetsu School of Flower Arranging, Courses 5-10, Wash
ington, D.C.:  M. OkadaCultural Services Association,
1982.

Magazines and Newspaper Articles:

Barber, Andrew, "Hope Never Dies in a True Gardener's
Heart," in Menninger  Perspective, Spring, 1980.

Frankl, Elizabeth, "Painting The Souls of Flowers," in East
West Journal of Natural Health & Living: May 1989.

Fujieda, Itsuki Okada, "The Vibration of the Daylight Age," in
The Glory, No. 58, Atami:  Church of World Messianity.

Gorman, Tom, "Art From the Inside," Los Angeles Times
Newspaper, December 5, 1988.

Lush, Jean, with Patricia Rushford,  "Women of Beauty and
the Essence of Mystique," in   Focus On The Family:
May, 1987. Article excerpt from her book, Emotional
Phases of a Woman's Life, Fleming H. Revell Co., Grand
Rapids, MI.

Odent, Michel, M.D., "The Evolution of Obstetrics at
Pithiviers, <u>Birth and The Family Journal.</u> Vol. 8,
Spring, 1981.

ZaJonc, Arthur G., "The Wearer of Shapes-Goethe's Study of
Clouds and Weather," <u>Orion Nature Quarterly</u>: Winter,
1984.

Lectures:

Gorter, Robert, M.D. "Threefold/Fourfold Man," August 29, 1987.

Gorter, Robert, M.D. "Anthroposophical Medicine," March 23,
1981.

Roel, Jannebeth, "Elementals, " July 18, 1987.

Unpublished Correspondence and Papers:

Long Beach Sangetsu Students Correspondence, received 1989.

Wakayama Women's Prison Inmates Correspondence, received
1989.

Roel, Jannebeth, " Goethe's Color Theory in the Twentieth
Century," unpublished paper, 1990. (including quotation
from Willem Zeylmans Van Emmichoven)

# Index

For Information regarding Sangetsu Classes in your area:

Sangetsu North America
1971 W. 190th Street, Suite 280
Torrance, CA 90504
fax 310/523-3843